How to Pass
the Life in the
UK Test

How to Pass
the Life in the UK Test

Succeed in your application for
naturalisation as a British citizen or
indefinite leave to remain

Chris Tyreman

LONDON PHILADELPHIA NEW DELHI

Publisher's note

Every possible effort has been made to ensure that the information contained in this book is accurate at the time of going to press, and the publishers and author cannot accept responsibility for any errors or omissions, however caused. No responsibility for loss or damage occasioned to any person acting, or refraining from action, as a result of the material in this publication can be accepted by the editor, the publisher or the author.

First published in Great Britain in 2010 by Kogan Page Limited
Reprinted 2011

Kogan Page Limited
120 Pentonville Road
London N1 9JN
United Kingdom
www.koganpage.com

**L323.
623**

© Chris Tyreman, 2010

The right of Chris Tyreman to be identified as the author of this work has been asserted by him in accordance with the Copyright, Designs and Patents Act 1988.

Crown copyright material is reproduced with the permission of the controller of HMSO and the Queen's Printer for Scotland.

© Crown copyright 2010.

British Library Cataloguing-in-Publication Data

A CIP record for this book is available from the British Library.

ISBN   978 0 7494 5723 5
E-ISBN 978 0 7494 5941 3

Typeset by Graphicraft Limited, Hong Kong
Print production managed by Jellyfish
Printed in the UK by CPI Anthony Rowe

Contents

Introduction to the test

If you wish to settle in the UK or become a British citizen, you must pass the 'Life in the UK Test'. The test checks your knowledge of life in Britain and your understanding of the English language (ESOL level 3 standard).

The questions in the test are based on the Home Office book *Life in the United Kingdom: A Journey to Citizenship*, published by The Stationery Office (TSO) April 2007, ISBN 9780113413133. The questions cover Chapters 2, 3, 4, 5 and 6 of the Home Office book.

Practice test 1, at the end of Chapter 1, covers all five chapters of the Home Office book. It will give you some idea of the types of questions you will meet in the test. Do not worry if you cannot answer the questions now; you can always return to the test later. The questions in Chapters 2 to 6 will help you to learn and remember the knowledge you need for the test. These five chapters are:

Chapter 2: A changing society (questions 1 to 96);
Chapter 3: UK today: a profile (questions 97 to 228);
Chapter 4: How the UK is governed (questions 229 to 348);
Chapter 5: Everyday needs (questions 349 to 511);
Chapter 6: Employment (questions 512 to 610).

After completing the questions in Chapters 2 to 6 you will be ready to answer the mixed questions in the five practice tests found in Chapter 8. Each practice test covers the range of knowledge found in the Life in the UK Test.

Answers to the questions are found at the end of the book. You can use the blank marking sheets to record whether you have answered the questions correctly (✓) or incorrectly (✗).

Taking the test

The Life in the UK Test is a computer-based test using a mouse and keyboard. There are 24 questions and you need to answer 18 questions correctly to pass (no more than six wrong answers). The time allowed for the test is 45 minutes, but most people finish it in less than 30 minutes. Be careful not to click on the 'finish test' button by mistake until you have answered all the questions.

Locate a test centre near to you by going to the Life in the UK Test website: http://www.lifeintheuktest.gov.uk/ or telephone 0800 0154245 to book a test. You will be offered a test within one to four weeks. At the time of writing the test fee was £34.

You MUST take photographic identification (ID), for example, a passport from your own country, a UK photo-card driving licence, an immigration status document with a photo, or a Home Office Travel document with a photo. You should also take a document that shows your postcode; for example, a bank statement, gas or electricity bill or a Home Office letter.

If you pass the test, which is marked by computer, the test centre will give you a certificate straight away. If you lose the certificate it will not be re-issued and you will have to apply to re-sit the test and pay another fee.

Information on British citizenship or permanent residence in the UK (also known as 'settlement' or 'indefinite leave to remain') is available from the Home Office UK Border Agency website: http://www.bia.homeoffice.gov.uk.

Practice test 1

1   There is a long history of immigration to the UK.

A. True   B. False

Answer ⬚

2   When was the First World War?

A. 1914–1918   B. 1939–1945

C. 1935–1939   D. 1945–1949

Answer ⬚

3   In Britain today, women are entitled to the same pay as men for doing the same job.

A. True   B. False

Answer ⬚

4   Which UK country has the smallest proportion of ethnic minority groups?

A. England   B. Wales

C. Scotland   D. Northern Ireland

Answer ⬚

5   From which country did immigrants come to Britain because of a potato famine?

A. Poland   B. Ireland

C. Scotland   D. France

Answer ⬚

6   In 1948 people were invited to come to Britain from where?

A. France   B. Germany

C. India   D. West Indies

Answer ⬚

7 In which region do people speak with a Geordie accent?

A. Liverpool   B. Manchester

C. Tyneside   D. London

Answer [   ]

8 What percentage of the UK population do NOT attend religious services?

A. 10%   B. 25%   C. 50%   D. 90%

Answer [   ]

9 After Christian, the next largest religious group in the UK is Muslim.

A. True   B. False

Answer [   ]

10 What do the letters GCSE stand for?

A. General Certificate of Standard Education

B. General Certificate of Secondary Education

C. General Certificate of School Education

D. Graded Certificate of Secondary Education

Answer [   ]

11 At what age can young people buy cigarettes and tobacco?

A. 16   B. 17   C. 18   D. 21

Answer [   ]

12 The 2001 census did not collect information on which ONE of the following?

A. Sexual orientation   B. Ethnicity

C. Religion   D. Occupation

Answer [   ]

13 Who is the head of the British Commonwealth?

A. Prime Minister   B. Prince Charles

C. The Queen   D. Chancellor of
                                  the Exchequer

Answer [ ]

14 How many countries signed the Treaty of Rome in 1957?

A. 2   B. 4   C. 6   D. 8

Answer [ ]

15 The European Parliament meets in Strasbourg and which other European city?

A. Berlin   B. London

C. Paris   D. Brussels

Answer [ ]

16 Most people in the UK live in rented accommodation?

A. True   B. False

Answer [ ]

17 Which TWO of the following countries do not use the Euro as their currency?

A. Ireland   B. France

C. Scotland   D. Northern Ireland

Answer [ ]

18 Children at private schools have some of their fees paid for by the Government.

A. True   B. False

Answer [ ]

19   A film with a Universal (U) classification is which one of the following?

A. Under parental   B. Unsuited
   guidance   to children

C. Age 4 years   D. Age 12
   and above   and above

Answer [   ]

20   If you and two other tenants share a house and you each have a TV how many television licences are needed?

A. 0   B. 1   C. 2   D. 3

Answer [   ]

21   What is the youngest age that a young person can drink wine or beer with a meal in a hotel or restaurant?

A. 14   B. 16   C. 18   D. 21

Answer [   ]

22   At what age can you drive a 125 cc motorcycle in the UK?

A. 16   B. 17   C. 18   D. 21

Answer [   ]

23   Who issues MOT certificates?

A. Ministry of Traffic   B. Ministry of Transport

C. Ministry of Trade   D. Ministry of Transportation

Answer [   ]

24   Which ONE of the following would you normally include with your CV (Curriculum Vitae) when applying for a job?

A. Covering letter   B. CRB check

C. Education   D. Work permit
   certificates

Answer [   ]

CHAPTER 2

A changing society

Migration to Britain ☑

- ☐ Why people come to Britain and where they come from.
- ☐ Who came to Britain, how many and what jobs they did.
- ☐ When and why immigration was encouraged.
- ☐ Which countries are in the Commonwealth.

The changing role of women ☑

- ☐ Changes in women's roles and in women's rights.
- ☐ Education, work, childcare and discrimination.

Children, family and young people ☑

- ☐ Young people in the UK and who they live with.
- ☐ When they attend school and what exams they take.
- ☐ Drug use and alcohol consumption.
- ☐ Work and leisure activities.

Migration to Britain

1   Britain has a tradition of offering safety to people who are escaping hardship or persecution.

A. True   B. False

Answer [   ]

2   Many people living in Britain today can trace their roots to which regions of the world?

A. Europe, Asia   B. Australia and
   and Africa   New Zealand

C. USA and Canada   D. China, Hong Kong
                           and Taiwan

Answer [   ]

3   In the distant past, why did people invade Britain?

A. To escape   B. To seize land
   persecution   and stay

C. To find work   D. For a better life

Answer [   ]

4   The Huguenots came to Britain in the 16th and 18th centuries to escape religious persecution in France.

A. True   B. False

Answer [   ]

5   The Huguenots were French Catholics.

A. True   B. False

Answer [   ]

6   In which decade did Irish immigrants come to Britain because of a potato famine?

A. 1840s   B. 1880s   C. 1920s   D. 1940s

Answer [   ]

7   Which TWO of the following did Irish labour help to build across Britain?

A. Roads   B. Railways   C. Canals   D. Cities

Answer [   ]

8   'Pogroms' were racist attacks especially on which people?

A. Irish   B. Catholic   C. Christian   D. Jewish

Answer [   ]

9   When did people come to Britain to escape 'Pogroms'?

A. 1920–1950   B. 1850–1880

C. 1880–1910   D. 1910–1930

Answer [   ]

10   In which countries were there 'Pogroms'?

A. France and   B. Poland, Ukraine and
   Germany   Belarus

C. Russia and   D. Poland, Austria and
   Afghanistan   Germany

Answer [   ]

11   The Second World War took place between which years?

A. 1914–1918   B. 1935–1939

C. 1939–1945   D. 1949–1955

Answer [   ]

12   After the Second World War, there was too little work and too many people to do it.

A. True   B. False

Answer [   ]

13   After the Second World War, from which TWO regions did the British government encourage workers to come to Britain.

A. Europe   B. Russia   C. Africa   D. Ireland

Answer [   ]

14 In which year were people from the West Indies invited to work in Britain?

A. 1942   B. 1944   C. 1946   D. 1948

Answer

15 In which decade was immigration from overseas encouraged because of economic growth?

A. 1950s   B. 1960s   C. 1970s   D. 1980s

Answer

16 For how many years did immigrants from the West Indies, India and Pakistan travel to work and settle in the UK?

A. 10   B. 15   C. 20   D. 25

Answer

17 The majority of immigrants from the West Indies, India and Pakistan worked in textile and engineering firms.

A. True   B. False

Answer

18 In which TWO areas of the country did the majority of immigrants from West Indies, India and Pakistan find jobs?

A. South East   B. South West

C. Midlands   D. Northern England

Answer

19 Where were centres set up to recruit people to drive buses in the UK?

A. India   B. Pakistan

C. West Indies   D. Bangladesh

Answer

20 In which decade did the UK government pass new laws to restrict immigration?

A. 1940s   B. 1950s   C. 1960s   D. 1970s

Answer

21 Immigrants from 'old' commonwealth countries had to face the new immigration laws.

A. True   B. False

Answer

22 Which TWO pairs are the 'old' commonwealth countries?

A. India and   B. Australia and
   Pakistan   New Zealand

C. Canada and   D. Bangladesh and
   South Africa   Nigeria

Answer

23 How many refugees were admitted from Uganda in 1972?

A. 280   B. 2,800   C. 22,000   D. 28,000

Answer

24 In the 1970s how many refugees from South East Asia were admitted into Britain?

A. 200   B. 2,000   C. 22,000   D. 220,000

Answer

25 In the 1980s the largest immigrant groups came from which TWO of the following countries?

A. India and   B. South Africa and
   Pakistan   New Zealand

C. Soviet Union   D. United States and Australia

Answer

26   In which decade did groups of people from the former Soviet Union first come to Britain?

   A. 1960s   B. 1970s   C. 1980s   D. 1990s

   Answer _____

27   Immigration in the UK is controlled by which one of the following government departments?

   A. Boundary   B. UK Border
       Commission   Agency

   C. DVLA   D. HM Revenue
                               & Customs

   Answer _____

28   Which one of the following are the main reasons for the global rise in migration since 1994?

   A. Escape religious   B. Education
       persecution   and training

   C. Food and water   D. Economic and
       shortages   political

   Answer _____

29   What are the main reasons why people come to Britain today?

   A. To escape religious   B. To claim
       persecution   benefits

   C. For safety, jobs   D. To rebuild
       and a better life   the country

   Answer _____

30   The UK includes England, Scotland and Wales but not Northern Ireland.

   A. True   B. False

   Answer _____

31   Which of these statements is correct?

A. Britain is attached to mainland Europe

B. Britain is an island

Answer [   ]

32   One in 10 people have a parent or grandparent born outside of the UK.

A. True   B. False

Answer [   ]

The changing role of women

33   Families were usually small in the 19th century.

A. True   B. False

Answer [   ]

34   In the 19th century, in poorer homes, men, women and children all contributed to the family income.

A. True   B. False

Answer [   ]

35   In the 19th century, women had as many rights as men.

A. True   B. False

Answer [   ]

36   In which year was a woman given the right to divorce her husband?

A. 1857   B. 1897   C. 1927   D. 1957

Answer [   ]

37   Up until which year did a woman's money and property automatically belong to her husband when she got married?

A. 1822   B. 1882   C. 1922   D. 1952

Answer [   ]

38   At the end of which century did women campaign for the right to vote?

A. 17th century   B. 18th century

C. 19th century   D. 20th century

Answer [   ]

39   Women who campaigned for the right to vote were known as:

A. Unionists   B. Ladettes

C. Actionists   D. Suffragettes

Answer [   ]

40   During the First World War women did not join the war effort.

A. True   B. False

Answer [   ]

41   At the end of the First World War, women over age 30 were given the right to vote and to stand for election to Parliament. When was this?

A. 1908   B. 1918   C. 1928   D. 1938

Answer [   ]

42   In which year were women given the right to vote at age 21, the same age as men?

A. 1908   B. 1918   C. 1928   D. 1938

Answer [   ]

43   During the First World War women did a variety of work.

A. True   B. False

Answer [   ]

44   In the early part of the 20th century, women were expected to leave their jobs when they got married.

A. True   B. False

Answer [   ]

45   Employment opportunities for women today are no better than they were in the past.

A. True   B. False

Answer [   ]

46   In which decades were Equal Pay and Sex Discrimination Laws passed?

A. 1920s and 1930s   B. 1940s and 1950s

C. 1960s and 1970s   D. 1980s and 1990s

Answer [   ]

47   What percentage of the workforce today is female?

A. 30%   B. 35%   C. 45%   D. 50%

Answer [   ]

48   There are more men than women at university.

A. True   B. False

Answer [   ]

49   Most boys leave school with better qualifications than girls.

A. True   B. False

Answer [   ]

50   In most households, women continue to have the main responsibility for housework and childcare.

A. True   B. False

Answer [   ]

51   Most people in the UK believe that women should stay at home and not go out to work.

A. True   B. False

Answer [   ]

52   Roughly what fraction of women with school-age children are in paid work?

A. 1/10   B. 1/4   C. 1/2   D. 3/4

Answer [   ]

53   Women have equal access to promotion and better-paid jobs than men.

A. True   B. False

Answer [   ]

54   Women who are expecting a baby are entitled to antenatal care.

A. True   B. False

Answer [   ]

55   Today, women are expected to leave their job when they get married and have children.

A. True   B. False

Answer [   ]

56   What is the minimum amount of maternity leave that a woman in work is entitled to?

A. 26 weeks   B. 36 weeks   C. 46 weeks   D. 52 weeks

Answer [   ]

57   What is the *total* amount of maternity leave that a woman in work is entitled to?

A. 26 weeks   B. 36 weeks   C. 46 weeks   D. 52 weeks

Answer [   ]

58   How much paternity leave can fathers take?

A. 1 week   B. 2 weeks   C. 4 weeks   D. 8 weeks

Answer [   ]

59 Discrimination against women in the workplace still exists in the UK.

A. True   B. False

Answer _____

60 Which of the following is not a traditional area of female employment?

A. Healthcare   B. Teaching

C. Engineering   D. Secretarial

Answer _____

61 The average hourly pay for women is less than for men by:

A. 5%   B. 20%   C. 40%   D. 50%

Answer _____

62 It is NOT government policy to help people with childcare responsibilities to take up work.

A. True   B. False

Answer _____

Children, family and young people

63 How many million young people up to the age of 19 are there in the UK?

A. 5 million   B. 10 million   C. 15 million   D. 20 million

Answer _____

64 What fraction of the UK population are young people up to the age of 19?

A. one-tenth   B. one-eighth

C. one-quarter   D. one-third

Answer _____

65   What percentage of children lives with only one parent?

A. 5%   B. 10%   C. 25%   D. 50%

Answer

66   What percentage of children lives with stepparents?

A. 10%   B. 15%   C. 20%   D. 25%

Answer

67   Most children in Britain receive weekly pocket money from their parents.

A. True   B. False

Answer

68   There is evidence to show that child molestation by strangers is on the increase.

A. True   B. False

Answer

69   Only a few young people move away from home once they become adults.

A. True   B. False

Answer

70   In England, Wales and Scotland, at what age must children start school?

A. age 4   B. age 5   C. age 6   D. age 7

Answer

71   At what age do children in England go to secondary school?

A. 9   B. 10   C. 11   D. 13

Answer

72 English, maths and science are NOT compulsory school subjects.

A. True   B. False

Answer ⬚

73 At what age do school children first take GCSE exams?

A. 15   B. 16   C. 17   D. 18

Answer ⬚

74 The letters GCSE stand for General Certificate of School Education.

A. True   B. False

Answer ⬚

75 The General Certificate of Education at an Advanced Level (AGCEs) used to be called A-Levels.

A. True   B. False

Answer ⬚

76 How many AS (Advanced Subsidiary) units need to be completed for an AS level.

A. 1   B. 2   C. 3   D. 4

Answer ⬚

77 Three AS units make up one-half of an AGCE.

A. True   B. False

Answer ⬚

78 Standard Grade qualifications in Scotland are the same as which qualification in the rest of the UK?

A. GCSE   B. AS   C. AGCE   D. A-level

Answer ⬚

79   AGCEs are the traditional route to higher education.

A. True   B. False

Answer _____

80   What proportion of young people go on to higher education?

A. 1 in 2   B. 1 in 3   C. 1 in 4   D. 1 in 6

Answer _____

81   When do some young people take a 'gap year'?

A. After completing   B. Before starting
   GCSEs   AGCEs

C. Before starting   D. Before finding
   university   a job

Answer _____

82   At what age can young people choose to study at Colleges of Further Education or Adult Education Centres?

A. 16   B. 17   C. 18   D. 19

Answer _____

83   Many children find a part-time job while they are still at school.

A. True   B. False

Answer _____

84   How many children are at work in the UK at any one time?

A. 1 million   B. 2 million   C. 3 million   D. 4 million

Answer _____

85   Children can do any type of work and any number of hours.

A. True   B. False

Answer _____

86 It is NOT illegal to sell cigarettes to young people under age 16.

A. True   B. False

Answer [   ]

87 More boys smoke than girls.

A. True   B. False

Answer [   ]

88 Young people have to be over age 18 to buy alcohol in Britain.

A. True   B. False

Answer [   ]

89 Drinking too much alcohol at any one time is known as 'binge drinking'.

A. True   B. False

Answer [   ]

90 In Britain it is NOT illegal to be drunk in public.

A. True   B. False

Answer [   ]

91 There are on-the-spot fines to help control drunkenness in public.

A. True   B. False

Answer [   ]

92 You can legally possess heroin, cocaine, ecstasy, amphetamines and cannabis in Britain.

A. True   B. False

Answer [   ]

93 What proportion of young people has used illegal drugs at one time or another?

A. one-quarter   B. one-third

C. one-half   D. two-thirds

Answer [   ]

94 What proportion of the population as a whole has used illegal drugs at one time or another?

A. one-quarter   B. one-third

C. one-half   D. two-thirds

Answer [   ]

95 Young people can vote in elections when they are 18 years old.

A. True   B. False

Answer [   ]

96 What percentage of young people has taken part in fund-raising or collecting money for charity?

A. 20%   B. 30%   C. 40%   D. 50%

Answer [   ]

CHAPTER 3

UK today: a profile

Population ☑

- ☐ The number of people in the UK and its nations.
- ☐ What a census is and when it is taken.
- ☐ The main ethnic minorities and their populations.

The nations and regions of the UK ☑

- ☐ The languages and dialects spoken in the UK.

Religion ☑

- ☐ What religions are practised in the UK.
- ☐ The different types of Christian churches.
- ☐ Who the head of the Church of England is.

Customs and traditions ☑

- ☐ Who the Patron saint is where you live.
- ☐ What the main Christian festivals and holidays are.
- ☐ Which non-Christian festivals are recognised.
- ☐ Which sports are the most popular in the UK.

Population

97 How many people live in the UK?

   A. 61 million   B. 51 million   C. 41 million   D. 31 million

   Answer [   ]

98 What percentage of the UK population live in England?

   A. 94%   B. 84%   C. 74%   D. 64%

   Answer [   ]

99 What percentage of the UK population live in Scotland?

   A. 20%   B. 15%   C. 8%   D. 3%

   Answer [   ]

100 What percentage of the UK population live in Wales?

   A. 20%   B. 15%   C. 10%   D. 5%

   Answer [   ]

101 What percentage of the UK population live in Northern Ireland?

   A. 15%   B. 8%   C. 3%   D. 1%

   Answer [   ]

102 By what percentage has the UK population grown since 1971?

   A. 3.7%   B. 7.7%   C. 13.7%   D. 20.7%

   Answer [   ]

103 In some areas of the UK the population has declined in the last 20 years.

   A. True   B. False

   Answer [   ]

104 Which of the following areas of the UK have shown a decline in population.

A. No areas

B. South East and South West

C. Midlands

D. North East and North West

Answer [   ]

105 The UK has an ageing population.

A. True

B. False

Answer [   ]

106 Both the birth rate and the death rate are climbing in the UK.

A. True

B. False

Answer [   ]

107 The number of people aged 85 and over is at a record low.

A. True

B. False

Answer [   ]

108 There are more children under age 16 in the UK than people over aged 60.

A. True

B. False

Answer [   ]

109 A census collects statistics on age, place of birth, health and housing.

A. True

B. False

Answer [   ]

110 A census does not collect information on which one of the following?

A. Ethnicity

B. Occupation

C. Marital status

D. Income

Answer [   ]

111 How often is a census form sent out?

A. every 5 years   B. every 10 years

C. every 15 years   D. every 20 years

Answer

112 When was the first census taken?

A. 1701   B. 1801   C. 1901   D. 2001

Answer

113 When will the next census be?

A. 2011   B. 2015   C. 2017   D. 2019

Answer

114 A census was not taken during when?

A. The death of   B. The Brixton
    Prince Albert   riots

C. The Second   D. The Miner's
    World War   strike

Answer

115 What percentage of UK households have to complete a census?

A. 10%   B. 25%   C. 50%   D. 100%

Answer

116 The information in a census is available for everyone to see.

A. True   B. False

Answer

117 Which country in the UK has the smallest population?

A. England   B. Scotland

C. Wales   D. Northern Ireland

Answer

118 What is the population of Scotland?

    A. 1 million   B. 3 million

    C. 5 million   D. 10 million

                       Answer [_____]

119 What is the population of Wales?

    A. 1 million   B. 3 million

    C. 5 million   D. 10 million

                       Answer [_____]

120 According to the census, what percentage of the UK population is White?

    A. 80%   B. 86%   C. 92%   D. 98%

                       Answer [_____]

121 According to the census, what percentage of the UK population is from the ethnic minorities?

    A. 20%   B. 15%   C. 8%   D. 2%

                       Answer [_____]

122 According to the census, what percentage of the UK population is of Mixed origin?

    A. 0.2%   B. 0.8%   C. 1.2%   D. 2%

                       Answer [_____]

123 In which year did large numbers of people start to arrive in the UK from the new East European member states?

    A. 1974   B. 1984   C. 1994   D. 2004

                       Answer [_____]

124 About half of all people from ethnic minority communities were born in the UK.

    A. True   B. False

                       Answer [_____]

125 Almost half of all people from ethnic minority groups live in London.

A. True   B. False

Answer [   ]

126 People from ethnic minorities make up almost what fraction of the population of London?

A. one-eighth   B. one-quarter

C. one-third   D. one-half

Answer [   ]

127 What are the two largest Asian populations in the UK?

A. Indian and   B. Indian and
   Bangladeshi   Pakistani

C. Pakistani and   D. Indian and
   Bangladeshi   Malaysian

Answer [   ]

128 How many Indian people are there in the UK?

A. 0.3 million   B. 0.5 million   C. 0.7 million   D. 1.1 million

Answer [   ]

129 What percentage of the UK population is Indian?

A. 1.3%   B. 1.8%   C. 2.3%   D. 2.8%

Answer [   ]

130 How many Pakistani people are there in the UK?

A. 0.3 million   B. 0.5 million   C. 0.7 million   D. 1.1 million

Answer [   ]

131 What percentage of the UK population is Pakistani?

A. 1.3%   B. 1.8%   C. 2.3%   D. 2.8%

Answer [   ]

132 How many Bangladeshi people are there in the UK?

A. 0.3 million   B. 0.5 million   C. 0.7 million   D. 1.1 million

Answer

133 What percentage of the UK population is Bangladeshi?

A. 0.4%   B. 0.5%   C. 0.8%   D 1.0%

Answer

134 How many Black Caribbean people are there in the UK?

A. 0.2 million   B. 0.3 million   C. 0.5 million   D. 0.6 million

Answer

135 What percentage of the UK population is Black Caribbean?

A. 0.4%   B. 0.5%   C. 0.8%   D. 1.0%

Answer

136 How many Black African people are there in the UK?

A. 0.2 million   B. 0.3 million   C. 0.5 million   D. 0.6 million

Answer

137 What percentage of the UK population is Black African?

A. 0.4%   B. 0.5%   C. 0.8%   D. 1.0%

Answer

138 How many Chinese people are there in the UK?

A. 0.2 million   B. 0.3 million   C. 0.5 million   D. 0.6 million

Answer

139 What percentage of the UK population is Chinese?

A. 0.4%   B. 0.5%   C. 0.8%   D. 1.0%

Answer

140 How many people of Mixed origin are there in the UK?

A. 0.2 million   B. 0.3 million   C. 0.5 million   D. 0.6 million

Answer

141 According to the latest census what percentage of the people in England are from ethnic minority groups?

A. 1%   B. 2%   C. 5%   D. 9%

Answer [   ]

142 According to the latest census what percentage of the people in Wales are from ethnic minority groups?

A. 1%   B. 2%   C. 5%   D. 9%

Answer [   ]

143 According to the latest census what percentage of the people in Scotland are from ethnic minority groups?

A. 1%   B. 2%   C. 5%   D. 9%

Answer [   ]

144 According to the latest census what percentage of the people in Northern Ireland are from ethnic minority groups?

A. 1%   B. 2%   C. 5%   D. 9%

Answer [   ]

145 What proportion of people from ethnic minority groups were born in the UK?

A. 1/2   B. 1/4   C. 1/5   D. 1/10

Answer [   ]

146 What proportion of people from ethnic minority groups live in the London area?

A. 5%   B. 10%   C. 25%   D. 45%

Answer [   ]

147 Which areas of England do NOT have large ethnic minority populations?

A. Midlands and   B. Yorkshire and
   the North West   Humberside

C. London and   D. South West and
   the South East   the North East

Answer [   ]

The nations and regions of the UK

148 Most of the people in the UK live in the countryside.

A. True   B. False

Answer [   ]

149 John O'Groats is in the south-west corner of England.

A. True   B. False

Answer [   ]

150 Land's End is on the north coast of Scotland.

A. True   B. False

Answer [   ]

151 What is the distance from John O'Groats to Land's End?

A. 870 miles   B. 1,000 miles
   (1,400 km)   (1,600 km)

C. 2,000 miles   D. 2,500 miles
   (3,200 km)   (4,000 km)

Answer [   ]

152 The UK is a medium-sized country.

A. True   B. False

Answer [   ]

153 Local customs, types of food and language vary very little around the UK.

A. True   B. False

Answer [   ]

154 A Cockney dialect is spoken in which city?

A. London   B. Manchester   C. Liverpool   D. Newcastle

Answer [   ]

155 A Scouse dialect is spoken in which city?

A. London   B. Manchester   C. Liverpool   D. Newcastle

Answer [   ]

156 A Geordie dialect is spoken in which city?

A. London   B. Manchester   C. Liverpool   D. Newcastle

Answer [   ]

157 Gaelic is spoken in the Highland and Islands of Scotland.

A. True   B. False

Answer [   ]

158 One of the dialects spoken in Northern Ireland is called Ulster Scots.

A. True   B. False

Answer [   ]

159 The Welsh language is NOT taught in Welsh schools and universities.

A. True   B. False

Answer [   ]

Religion

160 The UK has only been a Christian society in recent times.

A. True   B. False

Answer [   ]

161 In the UK, people are NOT free to practise the religion of their choice.

A. True   B. False

Answer [   ]

162 According the to 2001 census, what percentage of the population said that they had a religion?

A. 10%   B. 25%   C. 50%   D. 75%

Answer [   ]

163 What percentage of religious people are Christians?

A. 10%   B. 40%   C. 60%   D. 70%

Answer [   ]

164 What percentage of the UK population attend religious services?

A. 10%   B. 40%   C. 60%   D. 70%

Answer [   ]

165 What percentage of the UK Christian population are Roman Catholics?

A. 10%   B. 40%   C. 60%   D. 70%

Answer [   ]

166 What percentage of the Northern Ireland population are Roman Catholics?

A. 10%   B. 40%   C. 60%   D. 70%

Answer [   ]

167 What are the UK's two largest non-Christian populations?

A. Muslim and Sikh   B. Jewish and Buddhist

C. Sikh and Hindu   D. Muslim and Hindu

Answer [   ]

168 What percentage of the UK population are Muslims?

A. 0.3%   B. 0.6%   C. 1.0%   D. 2.7%

Answer

169 What percentage of the UK population are Hindus?

A. 0.3%   B. 0.6%   C. 1.0%   D. 2.7%

Answer

170 What percentage of the UK population are Sikhs?

A. 0.3%   B. 0.6%   C. 1.0%   D. 2.7%

Answer

171 What percentage of the UK population are Buddhists?

A. 0.3%   B. 0.6%   C. 1.0%   D. 2.7%

Answer

172 What percentage of the UK population are Jewish?

A. 0.3%   B. 0.5%   C. 1.0%   D. 2.7%

Answer

173 What percentage of the UK population say that they have no religion?

A. 5.5%   B. 10.5%   C. 15.5%   D. 20.5%

Answer

174 The Church of England is called the Episcopal Church in which TWO of the following countries?

A. Scotland   B. Wales   C. USA   D. Northern Ireland

Answer

175 The Church of England is called the Anglican Church in other countries.

A. True   B. False

Answer

176 The Church of England is a Catholic Church.

    A. True   B. False

                                   Answer

177 In which century was the Church of England set up?

    A. 1300s   B. 1500s   C. 1700s   D. 1900s

                                   Answer

178 The monarch (king or queen) is the head of the Church of England and is only allowed to marry a Protestant.

    A. True   B. False

                                   Answer

179 The Archbishop of Canterbury is the spiritual leader of which church?

    A. Church of England   B. Catholic Church

    C. Presbyterian   D. Methodist Church
       Church

                                   Answer

180 The Presbyterian Church is the main church in which part of the UK?

    A. England   B. Wales

    C. Scotland   D. Northern Ireland

                                   Answer

181 Wales and Northern Ireland have established churches.

    A. True   B. False

                                   Answer

182 Who is the Patron Saint of England?

    A. St Patrick   B. St David

    C. St Andrew   D. St George

                                   Answer

183 Who is the Patron Saint of Scotland?

A. St Patrick   B. St David

C. St Andrew   D. St George

Answer [   ]

184 Who is the Patron Saint of Wales?

A. St Patrick   B. St David

C. St Andrew   D. St George

Answer [   ]

185 Who is the Patron Saint of Northern Ireland?

A. St Patrick   B. St David

C. St Andrew   D. St George

Answer [   ]

186 When is St George's Day?

A. 1st March   B. 17th March

C. 23rd April   D. 30th November

Answer [   ]

187 When is Saint David's Day?

A. 1st March   B. 17th March

C. 23rd April   D. 30th November

Answer [   ]

188 When is Saint Andrew's Day?

A. 1st March   B. 17th March

C. 23rd April   D. 30th November

Answer [   ]

189 When is Saint Patrick's Day?

A. 1st March   B. 17th March

C. 23rd April   D. 30th November

Answer [   ]

190 Saint Patrick's day in Northern Ireland is the only saints' day to be taken as a public holiday.

A. True   B. False

Answer

191 In England, Saint George's day is taken as a public holiday.

A. True   B. False

Answer

192 In addition to four public holidays, how many Bank Holidays does the UK have?

A. 1   B. 2   C. 3   D. 4

Answer

193 Which of the following statements is correct?

A. More people attend religious services in Scotland and Northern Ireland than in England and Wales.

B. More people attend religious services in England and Wales than in Northern Ireland and Scotland.

Answer

194 Baptists, Methodists and Quakers are Protestant Christian groups.

A. True   B. False

Answer

195 Bank holidays have religious or national significance.

A. True   B. False

Answer

Customs and traditions

196 The main Christian festivals are Christmas and Easter.

A. True   B. False

Answer

197   Most people spend Christmas Day at home and eat a special meal that often includes turkey.

A. True   B. False

Answer

198   Boxing Day is which day in December?

A. 24th   B. 25th   C. 26th   D. 27th

Answer

199   New Year's Eve is on 30th December.

A. True   B. False

Answer

200   The 31st December is known as what in Scotland?

A. St Andrew's day   B. Hogmanay

C. Guy Fawkes' Night   D. Hallowe'en

Answer

201   New Year is not celebrated in the UK.

A. True   B. False

Answer

202   Boxing Day, New Year's Day and Easter Monday are all Bank Holidays.

A. True   B. False

Answer

203   Customs and traditions from various religions are not recognised in the UK.

A. True   B. False

Answer

204   Eid ul-Fitr is a Muslim holiday at the end of Ramadan.

A. True   B. False

Answer

205 Diwali is an Indian festival.

  A. True   B. False

                                      Answer [   ]

206 Hanukkah is a Jewish festival.

  A. True   B. False

                                      Answer [   ]

207 Only festivals from Christian religions are explained to children at school.

  A. True   B. False

                                      Answer [   ]

208 Which of the following is celebrated on 14th February?

  A. Valentine's Day   B. Hogmanay

  C. Guy Fawkes'   D. Remembrance
     Night   Day

                                      Answer [   ]

209 On which day do people exchange cards and gifts with someone they admire or love?

  A. Valentine's Day   B. Hogmanay

  C. Guy Fawkes'   D. Remembrance
     Night   Day

                                      Answer [   ]

210 April Fool's Day is on April 2nd.

  A. True   B. False

                                      Answer [   ]

211 On April Fool's Day, people play jokes on each other until midday.

  A. True   B. False

                                      Answer [   ]

212 What time of year are chocolate eggs eaten?

    A. Christmas   B. Lent

    C. Easter   D. Pentecost

Answer [＿＿＿＿＿＿]

213 Mother's Day in the UK is celebrated on Mothering Sunday, three weeks before Easter.

    A. True   B. False

Answer [＿＿＿＿＿＿]

214 The first Monday in May is May Day Bank Holiday and the last Monday in May is Spring Bank Holiday.

    A. True   B. False

Answer [＿＿＿＿＿＿]

215 Which of the following is celebrated on 31st October?

    A. Valentine's Day   B. Hogmanay

    C. Guy Fawkes' Night   D. Hallowe'en

Answer [＿＿＿＿＿＿]

216 'Trick or treat' is a custom for children on which night?

    A. Guy Fawkes' Night   B. Hogmanay

    C. New Year's Eve   D. Hallowe'en

Answer [＿＿＿＿＿＿]

217 On which night of the year are fireworks set off at home or in a special display.

    A. October 31   B. November 5

    C. November 11   D. December 25

Answer [＿＿＿＿＿＿]

218 Which of the following is celebrated on 5th November?

A. Valentine's Day   B. Hogmanay

C. Guy Fawkes' Night   D. Remembrance Day

Answer [   ]

219 On which night of the year might people carry lanterns made out of hollowed out pumpkins with a candle inside?

A. October 31   B. November 5

C. November 11   D. December 25

Answer [   ]

220 On the 11th hour of the 11th day of the 11th month a two-minute silence commemorates which of the following?

A. St George's Day   B. Remembrance Day

C. Queen's birthday   D. Valentine's Day

Answer [   ]

221 On which day do people wear a red poppy flower?

A. St George's Day   B. Remembrance Day

C. Mothering Sunday   D. Valentine's Day

Answer [   ]

222 The Notting Hill Carnival takes place in which UK city?

A. Nottingham   B. Birmingham

C. London   D. Edinburgh

Answer [   ]

223 The UK has national teams for football and rugby.

A. True   B. False

Answer [   ]

224 England, Wales, Scotland and Northern Ireland do NOT have their own rugby team.

A. True   B. False

Answer [   ]

225 Which of the following is NOT a popular sport in the UK?

A. Football   B. Cricket

C. Rugby   D. Baseball

Answer [   ]

226 In which sport might a team win the FA cup?

A. Football   B. Cricket

C. Rugby   D. Golf

Answer [   ]

227 What is the Grand National?

A. Golf tournament   B. Horse race

C. Football match   D. Grand prix

Answer [   ]

228 Which tournament is held at Wimbledon?

A. Golf   B. Snooker

C. Darts   D. Tennis

Answer [   ]

CHAPTER 4

How the UK is governed

The British Constitution ☑

☐ The role of the Queen.

☐ The UK government and its members.

☐ The devolved administrations.

☐ Elections and electoral systems.

☐ The judiciary, police, quangos and the media.

☐ Who can vote and stand for office.

The UK in Europe and the world ☑

☐ The European Union (EU), its members and aims.

☐ When the EU was set up and when the UK joined.

☐ Where the European Parliament meets and what it does.

☐ When the United Nations was set up and what it does.

The British Constitution

229 Parliament consists of which TWO of the following?

A. House of Commons   B. Judiciary

C. House of Lords   D. Monarchy

Answer [   ]

230 The UK is governed by a wide range of institutions.

A. True   B. False

Answer [   ]

231 Scotland, Wales and Northern Ireland do NOT have devolved administrations.

A. True   B. False

Answer [   ]

232 The British Constitution is written down in a single document.

A. True   B. False

Answer [   ]

233 The UK is a constitutional democracy with the Queen as the Head of State.

A. True   B. False

Answer [   ]

234 Queen Elizabeth II has reigned on the throne since when?

A. 1942   B. 1952   C. 1962   D. 1972

Answer [   ]

235 Queen Elizabeth II is the Head of State of which TWO of the following countries?

A. Denmark   B. Ireland   C. Australia   D. Canada

Answer [   ]

236 Denmark, Sweden, Norway and the Netherlands have a constitutional monarchy similar to the UK.

A. True   B. False

Answer [＿＿＿＿＿]

237 A constitutional monarchy means that the king or queen rules the country and makes the decisions.

A. True   B. False

Answer [＿＿＿＿＿]

238 The Queen cannot advise, warn or encourage the Prime Minister.

A. True   B. False

Answer [＿＿＿＿＿]

239 The opening of a new parliament each year is the role of who?

A. Prime Minister   B. Chancellor

C. The Queen   D. Speaker of
                             the House

Answer [＿＿＿＿＿]

240 The Queen's speech summarizes which of the following for the year ahead?

A. European Laws   B. Cabinet decisions

C. Role of the   D. Government policies
   monarchy

Answer [＿＿＿＿＿]

241 Who is the Queen's eldest son?

A. Prince Edward   B. Prince Harry

C. Prince Andrew   D. Prince Charles

Answer [＿＿＿＿＿]

242 Who is the heir to the throne?

   A. Prince Edward   B. Prince Harry

   C. Prince Andrew   D. Prince Charles

                                    Answer

243 Prince Charles is the Prince of which country?

   A. England   B. Ireland

   C. Scotland   D. Wales

                                    Answer

244 The UK government is chosen by the people in democratic elections.

   A. True   B. False

                                    Answer

245 The decisions on Government policies are made by the Prime Minister and Cabinet.

   A. True   B. False

                                    Answer

246 A General Election has to be held at least once every

   A. 5 years   B. 4 years

   C. 3 years   D. 2 years

                                    Answer

247 What is a parliamentary constituency?

   A. A political party   B. A ceremonial role

   C. A voting system   D. An area of the country

                                    Answer

248 Each constituency elects two members of Parliament.

   A. True   B. False

                                    Answer

249 Members of Parliament (MPs) are elected through a system known as:

A. First shall   B. First in
   be last   last out

C. First past   D. First come
   the post   first served

Answer

250 To become a Member of Parliament a person must win the majority of votes in the constituency.

A. True   B. False

Answer

251 To become a Member of Parliament a person must win the highest number of votes in the constituency.

A. True   B. False

Answer

252 The party with the highest number of votes is the one that forms the government.

A. True   B. False

Answer

253 The party that wins the majority of constituencies is the one that forms the government.

A. True   B. False

Answer

254 How many Members of Parliament (MPs) are there in the UK?

A. 446   B. 546

C. 646   D. 746

Answer

255 When does a by-election take place?

A. When Parliament opens

B. Every 5 years

C. When an MP dies or resigns

D. At a General Election

Answer

256 The MPs responsible for party discipline and attendance are called what?

A. Speakers   B. Peers   C. Whips   D. Ministers

Answer

257 Elections to the European Parliament are held every how many years?

A. 2   B. 3   C. 4   D. 5

Answer

258 How many seats has the UK in the European Parliament?

A. 38   B. 58   C. 78   D. 108

Answer

259 An MEP is a member of the English Parliament.

A. True   B. False

Answer

260 What system of voting is used in elections to the European Parliament?

A. First past the post   B. Proportional representation

C. One winner   D. Majority rule

Answer

261 In proportional representation (PR) a party that wins 75% of the votes will receive what proportion of the seats?

A. 0%   B. 50%   C. 75%   D. 100%

Answer

262 Members of the House of Lords are democratically elected.

A. True   B. False

Answer [   ]

263 Members of the House of Lords are known as:

A. Speakers   B. Peers   C. Whips   D. Ministers

Answer [   ]

264 Since when has the Prime Minister had the power to appoint peers?

A. 1948   B. 1958   C. 1968   D. 1978

Answer [   ]

265 Until 1958 all peers were either hereditary or senior judges or bishops.

A. True   B. False

Answer [   ]

266 The House of Lords is more important than the House of Commons.

A. True   B. False

Answer [   ]

267 Members of the general public are not allowed into the House of Commons or the House of Lords.

A. True   B. False

Answer [   ]

268 The House of Lords approves and amends new laws (Bills).

A. True   B. False

Answer [   ]

269 The House of Lords might not agree to pass a law for which the House of Commons has voted.

A. True   B. False

Answer

270 The Prime Minister (PM) is the leader of the party in office and appoints the members of the Cabinet.

A. True   B. False

Answer

271 Where is the official home of the Prime Minister?

A. 11 Downing Street   B. Chequers

C. Houses of   D. 10 Downing Street
   Parliament

Answer

272 What is the name of the Prime Minister's country home not far from London?

A. 11 Downing Street   B. Chequers

C. Parliament House   D. 10 Downing Street

Answer

273 The Prime Minister usually stays on as leader if his or her party is defeated in a general election.

A. True   B. False

Answer

274 The official home of the Chancellor of the Exchequer is where?

A. 11 Downing Street   B. Chequers

C. Houses of   D. 10 Downing Street
   Parliament

Answer

275 The Chancellor of the Exchequer is responsible for

A. Economy   B. Law and order

C. Education   D. Defence

Answer

276 The Home Secretary is responsible for immigration and which other office?

A. Education   B. Law and order

C. Health   D. Defence

Answer

277 The Lord Chancellor is responsible for legal affairs.

A. True   B. False

Answer

278 What is the Cabinet?

A. A group of peers   B. A lobby group

C. A small committee   D. A pressure group

Answer

279 How often does the Cabinet usually meet?

A. Every day   B. Twice a week

C. Weekly   D. Monthly

Answer

280 Who makes important decisions about government policy?

A. Life peers   B. The Cabinet

C. The Speaker   D. The Opposition

Answer

281 The Shadow Cabinet is appointed by who?

A. Prime Minister   B. Leader of the Opposition

C. Secretary of State   D. Speaker of the House

Answer

282 How often does the Prime Minister come to the House of Commons to answer oral questions?

A. Daily   B. Weekly   C. Monthly   D. Yearly

Answer [   ]

283 The chief officer of the House of Commons is known as the

A. Chancellor   B. Minister   C. Whip   D. Speaker

Answer [   ]

284 Who chairs debates in the House of Commons and makes sure that rules are followed?

A. Life peers   B. The Cabinet

C. The Speaker   D. The Opposition

Answer [   ]

285 The Speaker is politically neutral.

A. True   B. False

Answer [   ]

286 Under the British system of democracy most citizens over age 18 can stand for election as a Member of Parliament (MP).

A. True   B. False

Answer [   ]

287 The three main political parties in the UK are the Conservative Party, the Labour Party and which other Party?

A. Independence   B. Liberal

C. Green   D. Plaid Cymru

Answer [   ]

288 'Independent' candidates do not represent any of the main political parties.

A. True   B. False

Answer [   ]

289 People are more likely to join a political party than to support a pressure group such as Greenpeace or Liberty.

A. True   B. False

Answer [   ]

290 Civil servants carry out government policy but have to be politically neutral.

A. True   B. False

Answer [   ]

291 Wales, Scotland and Northern Ireland have devolved governments.

A. True   B. False

Answer [   ]

292 In which year was the Scottish Parliament formed?

A. 1969   B. 1979

C. 1989   D. 1999

Answer [   ]

293 The Scottish Parliament cannot legislate on law, health and education.

A. True   B. False

Answer [   ]

294 In which city is the Scottish Parliament situated?

A. Edinburgh   B. Aberdeen

C. Glasgow   D. Dundee

Answer [   ]

295 An MSP is a member of the Scottish Parliament.

A. True   B. False

Answer [   ]

296 Members of the Scottish Parliament are elected by a 'first past the post system'.

A. True   B. False

Answer [   ]

297 Assembly Members (AMs) meet in the Senedd in which country?

A. Wales   B. Scotland

C. Northern Ireland   D. England

Answer [   ]

298 In which city is the Welsh Assembly Government situated?

A. Wrexham   B. Swansea   C. Cardiff   D. Newport

Answer [   ]

299 How many Welsh Assembly Members are there?

A. 20   B. 40   C. 60   D. 80

Answer [   ]

300 Elections to the Welsh Assembly are held every how many years?

A. 2   B. 3   C. 4   D. 5

Answer [   ]

301 In which city does the Northern Ireland Assembly meet?

A. Newry   B. Belfast

C. Cardiff   D. Londonderry

Answer [   ]

302 In Northern Ireland there is a Catholic minority and Protestant majority.

A. True   B. False

Answer [   ]

303 How many Members of the Legislative Assembly are there in the Northern Ireland Parliament?

A. 108   B. 208   C. 308   D. 408

Answer [   ]

304 The UK Government does not have the power to suspend the Northern Ireland Assembly.

A. True   B. False

Answer [   ]

305 Towns, cities and rural areas are governed by democratically elected councils also known as local authorities.

A. True   B. False

Answer [   ]

306 In which month are local elections for councillors held?

A. April   B. May

C. June   D. July

Answer [   ]

307 'Council tax' does not apply to rented properties.

A. True   B. False

Answer [   ]

308 The largest police force in the UK is the Metropolitan Police in London.

A. True   B. False

Answer [   ]

309 Where are the headquarters of the Metropolitan Police?

A. Fleet Street   B. New Scotland Yard

C. Covent Garden   D. Tower of London

Answer [   ]

310 Who make the laws in the UK?

  A. Police   B. Quangos

  C. Parliament   D. Judges

  Answer [   ]

311 A 'quango' is an organisation that is funded by the government but acts independently of the government.

  A. True   B. False

  Answer [   ]

312 A written record of what is said in Parliament is published in the Hansard report.

  A. True   B. False

  Answer [   ]

313 Newspapers are under Government control.

  A. True   B. False

  Answer [   ]

314 Citizens of EU states who are resident in the UK can vote in national parliamentary (general) elections.

  A. True   B. False

  Answer [   ]

315 In what year was the present voting age of 18 set?

  A. 1918   B. 1929

  C. 1969   D. 1999

  Answer [   ]

316 An electoral registration form is sent to every household in England and Wales.

  A. True   B. False

  Answer [   ]

The UK in Europe and the world

317 Which TWO of the following are true about the British Commonwealth?

A. The Queen is the head

B. It has power over its members

C. There are 23 members

D. It can suspend membership

Answer [   ]

318 Most of the countries in the Commonwealth were once part of the British Empire.

A. True   B. False

Answer [   ]

319 How many Commonwealth countries are there?

A. 23   B. 33   C. 43   D. 53

Answer [   ]

320 Australia, New Zealand and Canada are Commonwealth countries.

A. True   B. False

Answer [   ]

321 India, Pakistan and Cyprus are Commonwealth countries.

A. True   B. False

Answer [   ]

322 South Africa is not a Commonwealth country.

A. True   B. False

Answer [   ]

323 What are TWO aims of the Commonwealth?

A. Promote free trade   B. Eradicate poverty

C. Promote   D. Promote peace
   democracy   and security

Answer [   ]

324 The UK was one of the original six countries in the European Union (EU).

A. True   B. False

Answer [   ]

325 When was the European Economic Community (EEC) first set up?

A. 1949   B. 1957   C. 1972   D. 2001

Answer [   ]

326 What agreement did six European countries sign in 1957?

A. Treaty of Paris   B. Treaty of Versailles

C. Treaty of Lisbon   D. Treaty of Rome

Answer [   ]

327 In what year was the Treaty of Rome signed?

A. 1947   B. 1957   C. 1967   D. 1977

Answer [   ]

328 When did the UK join the EU?

A. 1958   B. 1968   C. 1973   D. 1995

Answer [   ]

329 How many new members joined the EU in 2004?

A. 4   B. 6   C. 8   D. 10

Answer [   ]

330 How many EU members were there in 2006?

A. 7   B. 10   C. 17   D. 27

Answer

331 The Council of Ministers is the governing body of the EU and passes EU law.

A. True   B. False

Answer

332 The Council of the European Union is usually called the Council of Ministers.

A. True   B. False

Answer

333 The Council of Ministers is composed of one government minister from each EU country.

A. True   B. False

Answer

334 The European Commission is the civil service of the EU and it proposes new EU policies and laws.

A. True   B. False

Answer

335 The European Parliament can refuse to agree to the European laws proposed by the European Commission.

A. True   B. False

Answer

336 The laws and decisions of the European Union are not legally binding in the UK.

A. True   B. False

Answer

337 Citizens of the European Union can work in any EU country without a valid passport or identity card.

A. True   B. False

Answer [＿＿＿＿＿＿＿]

338 People from Switzerland, Iceland and Norway do not have the same free movement rights as EU nationals.

A. True   B. False

Answer [＿＿＿＿＿＿＿]

339 In which city is the European Commission based?

A. London   B. Strasbourg

C. Berlin   D. Brussels

Answer [＿＿＿＿＿＿＿]

340 In which TWO cities does the European Parliament meet?

A. London   B. Strasbourg

C. Berlin   D. Brussels

Answer [＿＿＿＿＿＿＿]

341 The United Nations (UN) was set up after the Second World War to prevent war and promote peace and security.

A. True   B. False

Answer [＿＿＿＿＿＿＿]

342 In what year did the UN make a Universal Declaration on Human Rights?

A. 1948   B. 1958   C. 1968   D. 1978

Answer [＿＿＿＿＿＿＿]

343 The UN consists of at least how many countries?

A. 40   B. 90   C. 120   D. 190

Answer [＿＿＿＿＿＿＿]

344 The UK is not one of the five permanent members of the UN
Security Council.

A. True   B. False

Answer [   ]

345 How many members are there on the UN Security Council?

A. 5   B. 10   C. 15   D. 20

Answer [   ]

346 The UN is not concerned with human rights, children's rights
and discrimination against women.

A. True   B. False

Answer [   ]

347 The United States of America (USA) is part of the UN.

A. True   B. False

Answer [   ]

348 Which of the following is NOT an Agreement produced by the
UN?

A. Universal declaration of human rights

B. Convention on the elimination of all forms of
discrimination against women

C. UN Convention on the rights of the child

D. World agreement on the technical barriers to trade

Answer [   ]

CHAPTER 5

Everyday needs

Housing ☑

- ☐ How to buy or rent accommodation.
- ☐ Landlords and tenancy agreements; discrimination.

Services in and for the home ☑

- ☐ Water, electricity and gas; paying bills; Council tax.

Money and credit ☑

- ☐ Opening a bank account.
- ☐ Credit, debit and store cards; credit unions.
- ☐ Who is entitled to social security benefits.

Health ☑

- ☐ What the NHS is; what is free and what is paid for.
- ☐ Who GPs are, where they work and how to register.
- ☐ What to do/who to contact if you feel unwell.
- ☐ What to do if you are pregnant; who registers a birth.

Education ☑

☐ When children go to school and the types of school.

☐ What the different types of tests and qualifications are.

☐ What education is available beyond age 16.

Leisure ☑

☐ How films are classified according to age.

☐ Who needs a television licence.

Travel and transport ☑

☐ How to find information about trains, buses and coaches.

☐ How to get a driving licence.

☐ The importance of insurance, road tax and the MOT.

☐ What to do after a road traffic accident.

☐ Ways to prove your identity.

Housing

349 What fraction of the UK population owns their own home?

A. one-quarter   B. one-half

C. two-thirds   D. three-quarters

Answer

350 A mortgage for buying a home is a loan, paid back with interest, usually over 25 years.

A. True   B. False

Answer

351 Information about a mortgage for buying a home is available from which TWO of the following?

A. Estate agent

B. Building society

C. Solicitor

D. Bank

Answer [   ]

352 Islamic (Sharia) mortgages are available from some banks.

A. True

B. False

Answer [   ]

353 To buy a home in England and Wales you would visit an estate agent first.

A. True

B. False

Answer [   ]

354 In which one of the following can you NOT find details about homes for sale?

A. National newspapers

B. Local newspapers

C. Building societies

D. Websites

Answer [   ]

355 Which one of the following arranges for buyers to visit homes that are for sale?

A. Solicitor

B. Landlord

C. Estate agent

D. Lawyer

Answer [   ]

356 In England, a house buyer can make an offer below the asking price.

A. True

B. False

Answer [   ]

357 In Scotland, a house buyer can make an offer below the asking price.

A. True   B. False

Answer [   ]

358 Who represents the person selling their house or flat?

A. Estate agent   B. Building society

C. Solicitor   D. Bank

Answer [   ]

359 Estate agents represent the person buying the house or flat.

A. True   B. False

Answer [   ]

360 To buy a home in Scotland you would visit a solicitor first.

A. True   B. False

Answer [   ]

361 Who carries out legal checks on a house and the seller?

A. Estate agent   B. Building society

C. Solicitor   D. Bank

Answer [   ]

362 Who carries out checks on the condition of a home?

A. Solicitor   B. Surveyor

C. Estate agent   D. Local authority

Answer [   ]

363 Making an offer on a house 'subject to contract' means that you will lose money if you change your mind and decide not to buy.

A. True   B. False

Answer [   ]

364 If you take out a mortgage to buy a home you must insure it against fire, theft and accidental damage.

A. True   B. False

Answer

365 Rented accommodation is NOT available from which one of the following?

A. Private landlords   B. Housing associations

C. Shelter   D. Local authorities

Answer

366 'Council housing' is provided by local authorities.

A. True   B. False

Answer

367 A tenancy agreement is a legal contract between you and your landlord.

A. True   B. False

Answer

368 Landlords usually require a deposit, equal to one month's rent, which will be given back to you unless you damage the property.

A. True   B. False

Answer

369 A landlord can raise the rent at any time without your agreement.

A. True   B. False

Answer

370 A landlord can force you to leave the property without a court order.

A. True   B. False

Answer

371 Landlords cannot discriminate on the basis of sex, age, race, nationality or ethnic group.

A. True   B. False

Answer

372 Housing associations rent housing for profit.

A. True   B. False

Answer

Services in and for the home

373 Water is supplied to all UK homes free of charge.

A. True   B. False

Answer

374 All homes in the UK have electricity and most have gas.

A. True   B. False

Answer

375 There is only one supplier of gas and electricity in the UK.

A. True   B. False

Answer

376 The cost of water rates depends on the size of your house unless you have a water meter.

A. True   B. False

Answer

377 At what voltage is UK mains electricity supplied?

A. 110 v   B. 220 v

C. 240 v   D. 440 v

Answer

378 In an emergency situation you can dial 999 or 112.

   A. True   B. False

   Answer

379 With a bank account you can pay your fuel bills by 'standing order' or 'direct debit'.

   A. True   B. False

   Answer [   ]

380 You can open a bank account at the Post Office.

   A. True   B. False

   Answer [   ]

381 In some parts of the country your waste must be split into paper, glass, metal and plastic for recycling.

   A. True   B. False

   Answer [   ]

382 Local authorities receive all of their money from council taxes and none from the government.

   A. True   B. False

   Answer [   ]

383 Council tax can only be paid for in one payment and not in instalments.

   A. True   B. False

   Answer [   ]

384 If you live in England, Wales or Scotland, by how much will your council tax bill be reduced if only one person lives in the house or flat?

   A. 5%   B. 10%   C. 25%   D. 50%

   Answer [   ]

385 Your council tax bill depends on the number of people living in the house.

A. True   B. False

Answer [   ]

386 Council tax helps to pay for which TWO of the following?

A. Gas and electricity   B. Refuse collection

C. Telephone lines   D. Education

Answer [   ]

Money and credit

387 Bank notes come in £1, £5, £10, £20 and £50 denominations.

A. True   B. False

Answer [   ]

388 Which UK country does not have its own bank notes?

A. Scotland   B. Wales

C. England   D. Northern Ireland

Answer [   ]

389 Most EU countries use the Euro as their currency.

A. True   B. False

Answer [   ]

390 Northern Ireland uses the Euro as its currency.

A. True   B. False

Answer [   ]

391 The Republic of Ireland does not use the Euro.

A. True   B. False

Answer [   ]

392 In which year did 12 EU countries adopt the Euro as their common currency?

A. 2002   B. 2000   C. 1998   D. 1992

Answer [ ]

393 Which TWO of the following are required for you to open a bank account?

A. £100 deposit

B. Passport or driving licence

C. Household (utility) bill

D. Proof of employment

Answer [ ]

394 Which TWO of the following do NOT draw money from your bank account?

A. Debit card

B. Credit card

C. Cheques

D. Store card

Answer [ ]

395 You must take out insurance when you purchase which one of the following?

A. Mobile phone

B. Household furniture

C. Television

D. Car

Answer [ ]

396 Low cost loans are available from which one of the following?

A. Banks

B. Credit unions

C. Building societies

D. Post Offices

Answer [ ]

397 Help with benefits and debt is available from which TWO of the following?

A. www.direct.gov.uk

B. Credit unions

C. Citizens Advice Bureau (CAB)

D. Post Offices

Answer [ ]

398 People on a low income and the unemployed cannot claim Housing Benefit to help pay for the rent.

A. True   B. False

Answer [ ]

399 You can receive social security benefits even if you do not have a legal right of residence ('settlement') in the UK.

A. True   B. False

Answer [ ]

400 Which one of the following will NOT receive welfare benefits?

A. people on low income   B. older people

C. sick and disabled   D. employed

Answer [ ]

401 Which one of the following does not provide information on social security benefits?

A. Jobcentre Plus   B. Credit unions

C. Citizens Advice Bureau (CAB)   D. Post Offices

Answer [ ]

Health

402 What do the letters NHS stand for?

A. Nationwide Health Service   B. National Health Service

C. National Health System   D. Nationwide Health System

Answer [ ]

403 In which year was the NHS set up?

A. 1948   B. 1958   C. 1968   D. 1978

Answer [   ]

404 The NHS does NOT provide all UK residents with free health-care and treatment.

A. True   B. False

Answer [   ]

405 The letters GP stand for which of the following?

A. General   B. General
   Pharmacist   Physician

C. General   D. General
   Practitioner   Practice

Answer [   ]

406 Family doctors (GPs) work in surgeries and Primary Health Care Centres.

A. True   B. False

Answer [   ]

407 A list of local GPs can be found at which TWO of the following?

A. Library   B. Pharmacist

C. Accident and   D. Post Office
   Emergency

Answer [   ]

408 You can register with a doctor as a NHS patient at which one of the following.

A. Local health   B. Walk-in
   authority   centre

C. Accident and   D. The GP's
   Emergency   surgery

Answer [   ]

409 You should wait until you are ill before registering with a doctor.

A. True   B. False

Answer [   ]

410 You do not need a medical card to register with a doctor.

A. True   B. False

Answer [   ]

411 Doctors (GPs) never visit patients at home.

A. True   B. False

Answer [   ]

412 You have to pay for your treatment from the GP.

A. True   B. False

Answer [   ]

413 Travel vaccinations are normally free on the NHS.

A. True   B. False

Answer [   ]

414 You need a letter from your doctor to attend the Accident and Emergency (A&E) department of the nearest hospital.

A. True   B. False

Answer [   ]

415 A GP will write you a prescription if you need medicines.

A. True   B. False

Answer [   ]

416 You can collect your medicine by taking the prescription to a local pharmacy (chemist).

A. True   B. False

Answer [   ]

417 NHS prescription charges are NOT free in which one of the following cases?

A. Suffer from a listed medical condition

B. Aged 60 or over

C. Aged over 19 and in full-time education

D. Aged under 16

Answer [   ]

418 You will not have to pay NHS prescription charges if you receive Income Support, Jobseekers' Allowance, Working Families or Disability Tax Credit.

A. True

B. False

Answer [   ]

419 In which part of the UK are NHS prescription charges free for everyone?

A. England   B. Wales   C. Scotland   D. Northern Ireland

Answer [   ]

420 The local pharmacist (chemist) can give advice on medicines and on some medical conditions that are not serious.

A. True

B. False

Answer [   ]

421 NHS Direct is a 24-hour telephone service providing nurses' advice if you are feeling unwell.

A. True

B. False

Answer [   ]

422 Where can you NOT go to see a doctor or a nurse?

A. Surgery

B. Hospital A & E department

C. Pharmacist

D. NHS walk-in centre

Answer [   ]

423 Information about health services, medical conditions and treatments is available from the NHS Direct website.

A. True   B. False

Answer [   ]

424 In a medical emergency you should:

A. Contact your GP   B. Call 999 for an ambulance

C. Speak to NHS   D. See your local Pharmacist
   Direct   (Chemist)

Answer [   ]

425 Minor tests and treatments are carried out in hospital out-patient departments.

A. True   B. False

Answer [   ]

426 Patients who have to stay in hospital overnight are known as in-patients.

A. True   B. False

Answer [   ]

427 In-patients have to pay for their meals whilst in hospital.

A. True   B. False

Answer [   ]

428 NHS dental treatment is free for everyone.

A. True   B. False

Answer [   ]

429 You can get the name of a dentist at which TWO of the following places?

A. Hospital   B. Library

C. Doctor's surgery   D. Citizens Advice Bureau

Answer [   ]

430 In which TWO of the following cases can you visit an optician and have a free eye test?

A. Pregnant   B. On low income

C. Age 16 or under   D. Aged 60 or over

Answer [   ]

431 In which part of the UK are eye tests free?

A. England   B. Wales

C. Scotland   D. Northern Ireland

Answer [   ]

432 Where can you NOT get information on maternity and ante-natal services?

A. GP   B. Health visitor

C. Nursery   D. Local health authority

Answer [   ]

433 Within how many weeks after giving birth must the mother (or her husband) register a baby at the local Register Office.

A. 6 weeks   B. 4 weeks

C. 3 weeks   D. 2 months

Answer [   ]

434 Where can you get advice on contraception and sexual health?

A. Citizens Advice   B. National Childbirth
   Bureau   Trust

C. Patient Advice and   D. Family Planning
   Liaison Service   Association

Answer [   ]

Education

435 Education is free and compulsory in the UK.

A. True   B. False

Answer [   ]

436 The education system is the same in England, Scotland, Wales and Northern Ireland.

A. True   B. False

Answer [   ]

437 Parents are NOT responsible for making sure that their child goes to school.

A. True   B. False

Answer [   ]

438 Parents can be prosecuted if their child fails to attend school.

A. True   B. False

Answer [   ]

439 Primary education starts at age five in England, Scotland and Wales.

A. True   B. False

Answer [   ]

440 Primary education starts at age four in Northern Ireland.

A. True   B. False

Answer [   ]

441 Primary education finishes at age 11 in England, Wales and Northern Ireland.

A. True   B. False

Answer [   ]

442 Primary education finishes at age 12 in Scotland.

    A. True   B. False

Answer [   ]

443 Until what age does the secondary stage of education last?

    A. 15   B. 16   C. 19   D. 21

Answer [   ]

444 Young people can continue with their education until they are 18.

    A. True   B. False

Answer [   ]

445 Secondary schools are smaller than primary schools.

    A. True   B. False

Answer [   ]

446 Most secondary schools are single sex.

    A. True   B. False

Answer [   ]

447 Most school children in the UK do not wear a school uniform.

    A. True   B. False

Answer [   ]

448 Parents do not have to pay for school uniforms and sports wear.

    A. True   B. False

Answer [   ]

449 There are no Muslim, Jewish or Sikh schools in the UK.

    A. True   B. False

Answer [   ]

450 Schools linked to a religion are known as 'faith schools'.

A. True   B. False

Answer [   ]

451 Private schools are also known as independent schools.

A. True   B. False

Answer [   ]

452 Parents pay the full cost of their child's education at private schools.

A. True   B. False

Answer [   ]

453 All state schools in England, Wales and Northern Ireland follow the National Curriculum.

A. True   B. False

Answer [   ]

454 Citizenship is part of the National Curriculum.

A. True   B. False

Answer [   ]

455 For how many days a year must a school be open?

A. 190   B. 220   C. 260   D. 365

Answer [   ]

456 Most university students in the UK do not have to pay their tuition fees.

A. True   B. False

Answer [   ]

457 In what TWO ways can a family on low income get help with a student's tuition fees?

A. Loan   B. Grant   C. Bursary   D. Income support

Answer [   ]

458   When students finish university and find a job they must pay their student loan back to the bank.

A. True   B. False

Answer [   ]

Leisure

459   Information about cinemas can be found in local newspapers and libraries.

A. True   B. False

Answer [   ]

460   A film with a U (Universal) classification is suitable for children of all ages.

A. True   B. False

Answer [   ]

461   If you watch television (TV) in your own room in a shared house you do not need to buy a TV licence.

A. True   B. False

Answer [   ]

462   People over age 75 can apply for a free TV licence.

A. True   B. False

Answer [   ]

463   Anyone in the UK with a TV or any equipment for watching or recording TV must have a television licence.

A. True   B. False

Answer [   ]

464   How long does a TV licence last for?

A. 12 months   B. 2 years   C. 5 years   D. 10 years

Answer [   ]

465 It is legal for children aged 16 to buy alcohol and cigarettes.

A. True   B. False

Answer [   ]

466 How old must you be to drink alcohol in a public house?

A. Age 16   B. Age 17

C. Age 18   D. Age 21

Answer [   ]

467 A landlord may allow children of 14 to enter a pub but they are not allowed to drink alcohol.

A. True   B. False

Answer [   ]

468 Most pubs in the UK close at 11 pm (2300 hrs).

A. True   B. False

Answer [   ]

469 Young people age 16 and 17 can drink wine or beer with a meal in a hotel or restaurant.

A. True   B. False

Answer [   ]

470 You can buy alcohol in a supermarket or off-licence at age 16.

A. True   B. False

Answer [   ]

471 You cannot receive an on-the-spot fine for being drunk in public.

A. True   B. False

Answer [   ]

472 Young people under 18 are allowed into betting shops or gambling clubs.

A. True   B. False

Answer [   ]

473 Children under 16 are allowed to buy lottery tickets and scratch cards.

A. True   B. False

Answer [   ]

474 A dog in a public place must wear a dog collar showing the name and address of the owner.

A. True   B. False

Answer [   ]

475 Dog owners do NOT have to clean up any mess the dog makes.

A. True   B. False

Answer [   ]

Travel and transport

476 Which one of the following websites does NOT provide information on public transport?

A. www.nationalrail.co.uk   B. www.citylink.co.uk

C. www.businesslink.gov.uk   D. www.translink.co.uk

Answer [   ]

477 Tickets do not usually have to be bought before you get on a train.

A. True   B. False

Answer [   ]

478 Students, families, people under age 26 and over 60 can buy discount train tickets.

A. True   B. False

Answer

479 At what age can you drive a car or motorcycle?

A. 16   B. 17   C. 18   D. 21

Answer

480 At what age can you drive a medium-sized lorry?

A. 16   B. 17   C. 18   D. 21

Answer

481 At what age can you drive a large lorry or minibus?

A. 16   B. 17   C. 18   D. 21

Answer

482 You must hold a driving licence to drive on the road.

A. True   B. False

Answer

483 A learner driver can drive a car without a provisional licence.

A. True   B. False

Answer

484 If you hold a provisional driving licence you can drive a motorcycle up to what engine size?

A. 50 cc   B. 125 cc   C. 250 cc   D. 500 cc

Answer

485 From which one of the following places can you get an application form for a provisional driving licence?

A. Post Office   B. Library

C. Driving instructor   D. Ministry of Transport

Answer

486 A learner driver must be with someone who is over age 21 and has held a full licence for more than three years.

A. True   B. False

Answer [   ]

487 Learner drivers must put on L plates and they cannot drive on motorways.

A. True   B. False

Answer [   ]

488 In which country can learner drivers put on D plates instead of L plates if they wish?

A. England   B. Wales   C. Scotland   D. Northern Ireland

Answer [   ]

489 In which country must a newly qualified driver display an R-plate for one year?

A. England   B. Wales   C. Scotland   D. Northern Ireland

Answer [   ]

490 How many stages are involved in getting a full driving licence?

A. 1   B. 2   C. 3   D. 4

Answer [   ]

491 If you have a provisional driving licence then pass a theory test and a practical driving test you will get a full driving licence.

A. True   B. False

Answer [   ]

492 After what age must drivers renew their driving licences every three years?

A. age 60   B. age 65   C. age 70   D. age 75

Answer [   ]

493 How long is a driving licence from a non-EU country valid for?

A. 1 month

B. 3 months

C. 6 months

D. 12 months

Answer

494 A driving licence from Iceland, Liechtenstein or Norway is NOT valid in the UK.

A. True

B. False

Answer

495 Which one of the following documents is NOT required to drive a car in the UK?

A. Vehicle log book

B. Road tax disc

C. Motor insurance

D. MOT certificate

Answer

496 Your car can be clamped, towed away or even crushed if you do not pay the road tax.

A. True

B. False

Answer

497 Your insurance is valid if you do not have a Ministry of Transport (MOT) test certificate.

A. True

B. False

Answer

498 From which one of the following can you get an MOT certificate from?

A. Post Office

B. Approved garage

C. Insurance company

D. DVLA

Answer

499 Not everyone in a vehicle has to wear a seat belt.

A. True   B. False

Answer

500 Children age 12 or above can use an adult seat belt.

A. True   B. False

Answer

501 Motorcyclists and their passengers do NOT have to wear crash helmets.

A. True   B. False

Answer

502 Sikh men with turbans do not have to wear crash helmets when riding on motorcycles.

A. True   B. False

Answer

503 You can hold a mobile phone while driving a car.

A. True   B. False

Answer

504 What is the speed limit on motorways and dual carriageways?

A. 50 mph   B. 60 mph   C. 70 mph   D. 80 mph

Answer

505 What is the speed limit on single carriageways?

A. 50 mph   B. 60 mph   C. 70 mph   D. 80 mph

Answer

506 What is the speed limit in built up areas?

A. 50 mph   B. 60 mph   C. 30 mph   D. 20 mph

Answer

507 If you are involved in a car accident with another vehicle and nobody is hurt, which one of the following do you NOT need to do?

A. Exchange names and addresses

B. Exchange insurance details

C. Call the police on 999 or 112

D. Contact your insurance company

Answer

508 UK citizens need to carry an identity (ID) card.

A. True

B. False

Answer

509 You may have to prove your identity when you do which TWO of the following?

A. Open a bank account

B. Buy a car

C. Buy a train ticket

D. Rent accommodation

Answer

510 You may have to prove your identity when you do which TWO of the following?

A. Insure a car

B. Hire a car

C. Apply for benefits

D. Apply for a job

Answer

511 If you have to prove your identity, which ONE of the following documents could NOT be used?

A. Passport

B. Driving licence

C. Fuel bill

D. Curriculum vitae (CV)

Answer

CHAPTER 6

Employment

Looking for work ☑

- ☐ Who can work; CVs, referees and CRB checks.

Equal rights and discrimination ☑

- ☐ Types of discrimination and where to get help.

At work ☑

- ☐ Your contract, pay and conditions.
- ☐ Your pay slip (tax, National Insurance); pensions.
- ☐ Problems at work; losing your job.

Working for yourself ☑

- ☐ Self employment: who to inform; records to keep.

Childcare and children at work ☑

- ☐ Maternity pay, paternity leave and childcare.
- ☐ Restrictions on children working.

Looking for work

512 Who provides guidance on who can work in the UK?

A. Jobcentres Plus   B. Employment agencies

C. NARIC   D. Home Office

Answer [   ]

513 Anyone can work in the UK and nobody ever needs a work permit.

A. True   B. False

Answer [   ]

514 Which one of the following does NOT advertise jobs?

A. Job centres   B. Employment agencies

C. Shop windows   D. Home Office

Answer [   ]

515 Anyone who wants to work in the UK needs a National Insurance (NI) number.

A. True   B. False

Answer [   ]

516 To apply for a National Insurance (NI) number you should phone which one of the following?

A. Customs and Immigration   B. Jobcentre Plus

C. HM Revenue & Customs   D. Citizens Advice Bureau

Answer [   ]

517 Which one of the following cannot be used as evidence of your identity when applying for a National Insurance (NI) number?

A. EU country passport   B. Immigration Status Document

C. Work Permit UK   D. Photo driving licence

Answer [   ]

518 Information on how overseas qualifications compare with UK qualifications is available from which one of the following?

A. Job centre   B. Home Office

C. ACAS   D. NARIC

Answer [   ]

519 Many job applications require that you send which TWO of the following?

A. Employer's   B. Curriculum
   report   Vitae (CV)

C. CRB check   D. Covering letter

Answer [   ]

520 Which one of the following is not on a Curriculum Vitae (CV)?

A. Education   B. Qualifications

C. Religious   D. Previous
   beliefs   employment

Answer [   ]

521 Referees for job applications are NOT normally which TWO of the following.

A. Personal   B. Members of
   friends   your family

C. Previous   D. Professional
   employers   people

Answer [   ]

522 If you want to work as a nurse or with children you will need a Criminal Record Bureau (CRB) check?

A. True   B. False

Answer [   ]

523 Information on CRB checks is available from the Police Force.

A. True   B. False

Answer

524 The Criminal Record Bureau (CRB) is an agency of the Home Office.

A. True   B. False

Answer

525 Information on English Language training is NOT available from which one of the following?

A. Job centre   B. www.learndirect.co.uk

C. Local library   D. Local college

Answer

Equal rights and discrimination

526 Employers can discriminate against their employees on the basis of which of the following?

A. age   B. qualifications

C. disability   D. nationality

Answer

527 Sex discrimination does not apply when the job involves working for someone in their own home.

A. True   B. False

Answer

528 In Northern Ireland you cannot be discriminated against on the grounds of your religion or political opinion.

A. True   B. False

Answer

529 Which Commission helps with sex discrimination at work?

A. Equality and Human Rights Commission

B. Commission for Gender Equality

C. Equality and Diversity Commission

D. Commission for Racial Equality

Answer

530 A woman doing the same job as a man will receive less pay.

A. True

B. False

Answer

531 Which ONE of the following is not an example of sexual harassment at work?

A. Indecent remarks

B. Bullying because of your sex

C. Inappropriate touching

D. Women receiving less pay

Answer

532 In which year did age discrimination at work become unlawful in the UK?

A. 1976   B. 1986   C. 1996   D. 2006

Answer

At work

533 Only employers and not employees are responsible for safety in the workplace.

A. True

B. False

Answer

534 An employee must be given a written contract of terms and conditions of work within how many months of starting a job?

A. 1 month   B. 2 months

C. 3 months   D. 6 months

Answer [   ]

535 Your employer does not have to give you a pay-slip with your wages.

A. True   B. False

Answer [   ]

536 Employees are entitled to holidays and sick pay.

A. True   B. False

Answer [   ]

537 The UK does not have a minimum wage.

A. True   B. False

Answer [   ]

538 Workers aged 22 and above receive a higher minimum wage than workers aged 16–21.

A. True   B. False

Answer [   ]

539 The minimum wage for 16–17 year olds is the same as for 18–21 year olds.

A. True   B. False

Answer [   ]

540 Your employer can ask you to work more hours than you are contracted for (overtime) but you do not have to do it.

A. True   B. False

Answer [   ]

541 Most employees over age 16 are entitled to at least how many weeks paid holiday every year?

A. 2 weeks   B. 3 weeks

C. 4 weeks   D. 5 weeks

Answer

542 Your pay-slip must show your tax (PAYE) and National Insurance contributions (NIC).

A. True   B. False

Answer

543 National Insurance (NI) helps to pay for the National Health Service (NHS) and State Retirement Pensions.

A. True   B. False

Answer

544 Your employer does not pay your National Insurance Contributions (NIC).

A. True   B. False

Answer

545 An employer can stop you from joining a Trade Union.

A. True   B. False

Answer

546 You can be dismissed from work without a warning if you are unacceptably late or cannot do your job properly.

A. True   B. False

Answer

547 You can be dismissed from your work immediately for serious misconduct.

A. True   B. False

Answer

548 If you are dismissed from work unfairly how long have you to make a complaint?

A. 1 month   B. 2 months   C. 3 months   D. 4 months

Answer

549 Most people who become unemployed can claim which of the following?

A. Income support   B. Jobseekers allowance

C. Working tax credit   D. Disability living allowance

Answer

550 Which TWO of the following organizations can help you with problems at work?

A. CRB   B. CAB   C. ACAS   D. NARIC

Answer

551 If you are made redundant at work your redundancy pay will depend on which TWO of the following?

A. Length of service   B. Your age

C. Your sex   D. Number of employees

Answer

552 Jobcentre Plus is run by which Government Department?

A. Work and   B. HM Treasury
   Pensions

C. Home Office   D. Transport

Answer

553 What is the state retirement age for men?

A. 55   B. 60   C. 65   D. 70

Answer

554 What is the current state retirement age for women?

A. 55   B. 60   C. 65   D. 70

Answer

Working for yourself

555 'New Deal' is aimed at which group of people?

A. New business

B. Young people

C. Unemployed

D. Immigrants

Answer

556 Self-employed people need to register for tax and National Insurance (NI) by telephoning which of the following?

A. VAT office

B. Customs and Immigration

C. Department of Pensions

D. HM Revenue & Customs

Answer

557 Self-employed people are NOT responsible for paying their own tax and National Insurance Contributions (NIC).

A. True

B. False

Answer

558 Self-employed people who make a small profit will have to pay which class of National Insurance Contributions (NICs)?

A. Class 1　　B. Class 2　　C. Class 3　　D. Class 4

Answer

559 Self-employed people who make a large profit will have to pay which TWO classes of National Insurance Contributions (NICs)?

A. Class 1　　B. Class 2　　C. Class 3　　D. Class 4

Answer

560 If you receive a tax return from HM Revenue & Customs either you or your accountant must complete and return it.

A. True

B. False

Answer

561 The state retirement age for women will increase gradually from 2010 to 2020 to make it the same as men.

A. True   B. False

Answer [   ]

562 Help on starting a business is available from which TWO of the following?

A. Job centre   B. Banks

C. Business Link   D. Citizens Advice Bureau

Answer [   ]

563 British citizens cannot work in any country that is a member of the European Economic Area (EEA).

A. True   B. False

Answer [   ]

Childcare and children at work

564 How many weeks of maternity leave are women entitled to?

A. 13 weeks   B. 26 weeks

C. 39 weeks   D. 52 weeks

Answer [   ]

565 How many weeks of paternity leave are men entitled to?

A. 2 weeks   B. 3 weeks

C. 4 weeks   D. 6 weeks

Answer [   ]

566 The government does not help people with childcare responsibilities to take up work.

A. True   B. False

Answer [   ]

567 How many million children are there at work in the UK?

A. 1 million   B. 2 million

C. 3 million   D. 4 million

Answer   [   ]

568 What is the youngest age that a child can do paid work?

A. 12   B. 13   C. 14   D. 16

Answer   [   ]

569 The local authority has no duty to check whether children are being exploited.

A. True   B. False

Answer   [   ]

570 Children aged 14 to 16 are allowed to do heavy work.

A. True   B. False

Answer   [   ]

571 Children aged 14 to 16 can deliver milk, sell alcohol and cigarettes or medicines, and work in a kitchen or chip shop.

A. True   B. False

Answer   [   ]

572 Children aged 14 to 16 cannot work with dangerous machinery.

A. True   B. False

Answer   [   ]

573 Which TWO of the following are required before a child can do work?

A. medical certificate   B. work clothes

C. employment card   D. curriculum vitae (CV)

Answer   [   ]

574 During the school holidays, how many consecutive weeks break must a child have when they do not work?

A. 2 weeks   B. 3 weeks

C. 4 weeks   D. 5 weeks

Answer

575 What is the maximum length of time a child can work before they must take a one-hour rest break?

A. 2 hours   B. 4 hours

C. 6 hours   D. 8 hours

Answer

576 When can school children work?

A. during school time   B. before 7 am

C. after 7 pm   D. on Saturday

Answer

577 What is the most number of hours a child aged 14–16 can work in any school week?

A. 6 hours   B. 8 hours

C. 10 hours   D. 12 hours

Answer

578 Children cannot work for more than one hour before they start school or for more than two hours after they finish school.

A. True   B. False

Answer

579 What is the most number of hours that any child aged 14–16 can work on any school day or on Sunday?

A. 1 hour   B. 2 hours

C. 4 hours   D. 8 hours

Answer

580 Which TWO of the following part-time jobs are popular with children?

A. Delivering   B. Street
   newspapers   trader

C. Factory work D. Shop work

Answer [   ]

581 It is illegal for children aged 16 to sell medicines, alcohol, cigarettes and lottery tickets.

A. True   B. False

Answer [   ]

CHAPTER 7

Knowing the law

You will not be tested on 'Knowing the Law', Chapter 7 of the official publication. However, ignorance of the law is not a defence, so knowing the answers to the following questions will be of practical value. Laws relating to motoring and employment have been covered in earlier chapters.

The rights and duties of a citizen

582 In the UK you cannot smoke in public places or at work.

A. True   B. False

Answer [   ]

583 In the UK you can carry a knife for the purposes of self-defence.

A. True   B. False

Answer [   ]

584 Using abusive or insulting words in public because of a person's religion or ethnic origin is not a crime in the UK.

A. True   B. False

Answer [   ]

585 In the UK the police can stop and search anyone they think might be involved in a crime.

A. True   B. False

Answer

586 To report a crime that is not dangerous or life-threatening you should contact your local police station.

A. True   B. False

Answer

587 If you are stopped by the police you should give the officer which TWO of the following?

A. Name   B. Date of birth

C. Telephone number   D. Address

Answer

588 New Scotland Yard is the home of which police force?

A. Scottish Police   B. Northern Ireland
   Service   Police Service

C. Strathclyde Police   D. Metropolitan Police

Answer

589 Civil disputes including getting back money, personal injury claims and divorce are held in which court?

A. Crown   B. County   C. Youth   D. Magistrates

Answer

590 Small claims to settle minor disputes require a solicitor.

A. True   B. False

Answer

591 Who decides whether people are innocent or guilty of a serious crime?

A. Magistrate   B. Judge   C. Plaintiff   D. Jury

Answer

592 In which court does the jury decide the outcome of a criminal trial?

A. Crown   B. County   C. Youth   D. Magistrates

Answer

593 In the UK, apart from Scotland, minor criminal cases are dealt with in which court?

A. Crown   B. County   C. Youth   D. Magistrates

Answer

594 In the UK, apart from Scotland, serious criminal cases are dealt with in which court?

A. Crown   B. District   C. Sheriff   D. Magistrates

Answer

595 In Scotland, serious criminal cases are heard in the Sheriff's court and minor criminal cases are heard in the District court.

A. True   B. False

Answer

596 Free legal advice is available from which of the following?

A. Law centre   B. Small claims court

C. Citizens Advice   D. Yellow pages
   Bureau

Answer

597 If you are charged in connection with a crime you will have to pay for advice from the duty solicitor.

A. True   B. False

Answer

598 A divorce cannot take place during the first year of marriage.

A. True   B. False

Answer

599 Same sex couples can form civil partnerships that grant them similar rights to those of married couples.

A. True   B. False

Answer

600 In the UK no person can be forced to get married against his or her own wishes.

A. True   B. False

Answer

601 You have to be a member of Church to be married in the UK.

A. True   B. False

Answer

602 If a married person dies without making a will, the husband or wife will get none of their possessions.

A. True   B. False

Answer

603 When a child's parents are not married the mother has parental responsibility.

A. True   B. False

Answer

604 Parental responsibility for a child finishes when the child is 16 years old.

A. True   B. False

Answer

605 It is NOT against the law for a child under 16 to be left alone in the home.

A. True   B. False

Answer

606 The Young Citizen's Passport is a passport for people aged 14 to 19.

A. True   B. False

Answer

607 Military service in the UK has been compulsory since 1960.

A. True   B. False

Answer

608 Goods bought from the home by telephone, post or the internet can be returned within 28 days for a full refund.

A. True   B. False

Answer

609 The price shown on the label of new goods is the price that you can normally expect to pay.

A. True   B. False

Answer

610 It is a criminal offence to dump your rubbish anywhere.

A. True   B. False

Answer

CHAPTER 8

Practice tests 2 to 6

Please read Appendices 1 to 6 at the end of this book before you try the practice tests. These will help to boost your knowledge quickly in many key areas.

TIP: Use the Appendices as a revision tool before you sit the test.

Each of the following five practice tests contains 24 questions, which is the same as in the real test. You have 45 minutes to complete each test and the pass mark is 18 correct answers (75%).

Use a separate piece of paper to record your answers then use the answer sheets at the end of the book to mark them as either correct (✓) or incorrect (✗). Look again at the questions you have answered incorrectly; you may find that you are weak on one particular chapter. There is little to be gained in revising those chapters that you have answered well.

All the questions are based on the Home Office book *Life in the United Kingdom: A Journey to Citizenship*, 2007 edition, Chapters 2, 3, 4, 5 and 6. The questions in the real test will not be the same as those in the five practice tests but they will test the same knowledge, so if you can pass all five tests you can expect to succeed. Finally, go back to practice test 1 at the start of the book and try it again to see how much you have improved.

Practice test 2

1   From which country did immigrants come to Britain to help build railways and canals?

A. Poland

B. Ireland

C. Scotland

D. France

Answer

2   When was the Second World War?

A. 1914–1919

B. 1939–1945

C. 1935–1939

D. 1945–1949

Answer

3   Many people living in Britain today can trace their roots to Europe, Asia and which other continent?

A. Australia

B. North America

C. Africa

D. South America

Answer

4   Which of these statements is correct?

A. Nigeria and Pakistan are 'old' Commonwealth countries.

B. Australia and Canada are 'old' Commonwealth countries.

Answer

5   Suffragettes were women who campaigned for equal pay.

A. True

B. False

Answer

6   In which English city do people speak with a Scouse accent?

A. Liverpool

B. Manchester

C. Newcastle

D. London

Answer

7 What do the letters AS stand for on a pupil's exam certificate?

A. Alternative
   Schooling

B. Advanced
   Secondary

C. Advanced
   Subsidiary

D. Advanced
   Scholarship

Answer

8 In which country are Standard Grade qualifications the same as GCSEs?

A. England   B. Wales   C. Scotland   D. Northern Ireland

Answer

9 Which is the largest Asian population in the UK?

A. Indian   B. Pakistani   C. Bangladeshi   D. Malaysian

Answer

10 Which part of the UK has the highest percentage of Roman Catholics?

A. England   B. Wales   C. Scotland   D. Northern Ireland

Answer

11 In which of the following years was there a census of the population?

A. 1973   B. 1982   C. 1991   D. 2000

Answer

12 What proportion of the UK population is non-white?

A. 2%   B. 8%   C. 16%   D. 20%

Answer

13 The South West and North East of England have large ethnic minority populations.

A. True   B. False

Answer

14   Which country celebrates St George's day?

A. Northern Ireland   B. England   C. Scotland   D. Wales

Answer

15   What fraction of the UK population do not own their own homes?

A. One-quarter   B. One-third

C. Two-thirds   D. Three-quarters

Answer

16   Which one of the following countries does not use the Pound Sterling as its currency?

A. Northern Ireland   B. England

C. Scotland   D. Republic of Ireland

Answer

17   NHS prescriptions are free to everyone in the UK.

A. True   B. False

Answer

18   Which one of the following film classifications is suitable for children aged 4 years and over?

A. 12   B. U   C. R18   D. PG

Answer

19   It is legal for children aged 16 to sell alcohol and cigarettes.

A. True   B. False

Answer

20   In which one of the following cases can you apply for a free television (TV) licence?

A. Two people sharing   B. On income support

C. Over age 75   D. Registered blind

Answer

21   On what type of road is the speed limit 60 miles per hour (mph)?

A. Single carriageway   B. Dual carriageway

C. Motorway   D. Expressway

Answer [   ]

22   Which of these statements is correct?

A. EU driving licences are not valid in the UK.

B. Non-EU driving licences are valid for 12 months.

Answer [   ]

23   People from which one of the following countries need a Work Permit to work in the UK?

A. Latvia   B. Poland   C. Slovakia   D. Belarus

Answer [   ]

24   To apply for a National Insurance (NI) number you should phone HM Revenue & Customs.

A. True   B. False

Answer [   ]

Practice test 3

1   The United Kingdom (UK) means England, Scotland and Wales.

A. True   B. False

Answer [   ]

2   In the 1990s where did the largest immigrant groups come from?

A. Former Soviet Union   B. Old Commonwealth countries

C. United States   D. South East Asia

Answer [   ]

3 People came to Britain between 1880 and 1910 to escape religious persecution in the Ukraine, Belarus and which other country?

A. Austria   B. Germany

C. Switzerland   D. Poland

Answer [   ]

4 The population of England is greater than the combined populations of Wales, Scotland and Northern Ireland.

A. True   B. False

Answer [   ]

5 When were women aged over 30 given the right to vote?

A. 1914   B. 1918

C. 1922   D. 1928

Answer [   ]

6 On which day in December is Christmas Eve?

A. 24th   B. 25th

C. 26th   D. 27th

Answer [   ]

7 When do people wear a red poppy in the UK?

A. November 5th   B. November 11th

C. December 25th   D. March 11th

Answer [   ]

8 Since when has the Queen reigned on the throne?

A. 1952   B. 1962

C. 1972   D. 1982

Answer [   ]

9 Since when have there been a Welsh Assembly and a Scottish Parliament.

A. 1939 B. 1959 C. 1979 D. 1999

Answer

10 Which of the following is not a 'mandatory service' provided by a local authority?

A. Education B. Housing

C. NHS D. Rubbish collection

Answer

11 Queen Elizabeth II is the Head of State of which one of the following countries?

A. Sweden B. Monaco

C. Canada D. Belgium

Answer

12 Who is elected by proportional representation?

A. MPs B. MEPs

C. Cabinet D. House of Lords

Answer

13 Which parliament meets in Holyrood?

A. Welsh B. Scottish

C. Northern Ireland D. UK

Answer

14 About how many senior MPs does the Prime Minister appoint to become ministers?

A. 5 B. 10 C. 20 D. 50

Answer

15 When did six EU countries sign the Treaty of Rome?

A. 1947   B. 1952   C. 1957   D. 1962

Answer

16 Which one of the following film classifications is suitable for everyone but some parts might be unsuitable for children?

A. 12   B. U   C. R18   D. PG

Answer

17 How many countries adopted the Euro as their currency in 2002?

A. 4   B. 8   C. 12   D. 16

Answer

18 The UK has 'faith schools' for Muslim, Jewish, Hindu and Sikh children.

A. True   B. False

Answer

19 A mortgage to buy a house is normally paid back over how many years?

A. 5 years   B. 10 years   C. 15 years   D. 25 years

Answer

20 What is the name of the charity that works to save important buildings and countryside in the UK?

A. National Savings   B. National Geographic

C. National Archive   D. National Trust

Answer

21 A pub in the UK can stay open after 11 pm without a special licence.

A. True   B. False

Answer

22   What do the letters NIC stand for on an employee's pay-slip?

A. No Interest   B. National Insurance
Charged   Collected

C. National Insurance   D. National Insurance
Charges   Contribution

Answer [   ]

23   Most of the laws protecting people at work apply equally to people doing part-time or full-time work.

A. True   B. False

Answer [   ]

24   If you are dismissed from your job and wish to claim compensation, within how many months must an Employment Tribunal receive your complaint?

A. 1 month   B. 3 months   C. 6 months   D. 12 months

Answer [   ]

Practice test 4

1   The UK (United Kingdom) means England, Wales, Scotland and Northern Ireland.

A. True   B. False

Answer [   ]

2   What percentage of the UK population are black people?

A. 2%   B. 4%   C. 6%   D. 18%

Answer [   ]

3   When did immigrants from Ireland come to Britain to help rebuild the country?

A. 1840s   B. 1880s   C. 1940s   D. 1980s

Answer [   ]

4   When did the government restrict immigration to Britain?

A. Late 1940s   B. Late 1950s

C. Late 1960s   D. Late 1970s

Answer _____

5   When were women given the right to vote at age 21, the same as men?

A. 1914   B. 1918   C. 1922   D. 1928

Answer _____

6   Few women with school-age children are in paid work.

A. True   B. False

Answer _____

7   When are fireworks set off in the UK?

A. Robert Burns'   B. Hallowe'en
   Night

C. Remembrance   D. Guy Fawkes' Night
   Day

Answer _____

8   What do the letters AGCE stand for on a student's exam certificate?

A. General Certificate of Education at an Advanced Level

B. Advanced Grade Certificate of Education

C. Alternative Certificate of Education at an Advanced Level

D. Additional Certificate of Education at an Advanced Level

Answer _____

9   In the 2001 general election how many first-time voters used their vote?

A. 1 in 2   B. 1 in 5   C. 1 in 15   D. 1 in 20

Answer _____

10 What fraction of the UK population are children and young people up to age 19?

A. one-tenth

B. one-sixth

C. one-quarter

D. one-third

Answer

11 Which of the following is NOT a protestant Christian group?

A. Catholics   B. Baptists   C. Methodists   D. Quakers

Answer

12 How many weeks before Easter is Mothering Sunday celebrated?

A. 1   B. 2   C. 3   D. 4

Answer

13 Who makes a speech before the state opening of parliament that outlines government policies for the year ahead?

A. Prime Minister

B. Prince Charles

C. The Queen

D. Chancellor of the Exchequer

Answer

14 Where does the UK parliament meet?

A. Stormont   B. Holyrood   C. Senedd   D. Westminster

Answer

15 Who is elected by a 'first past the post' election system?

A. MPs   B. MEPs   C. Cabinet   D. House of Lords

Answer

16 You do not need a television licence to play DVDs on a TV or to record videos.

A. True

B. False

Answer

17 Refugees whose asylum applications have not been successful can still have a National Insurance number.

A. True   B. False

Answer ☐

18 How many independent schools are there in the UK?

A. 25   B. 250   C. 2,500   D. 25,000

Answer ☐

19 A person who writes a short report on your suitability for a job
is known as which one of the following?

A. A friend   B. A reference   C. A tutor   D. A referee

Answer ☐

20 In which part of the UK are NHS prescription charges free to
everyone?

A. England   B. Wales   C. Scotland   D. Northern Ireland

Answer ☐

21 Most school children in the UK wear a school uniform paid for
by their parents.

A. True   B. False

Answer ☐

22 What is the most hours a school child can spend delivering
newspapers on any school day or on Sunday?

A. 12   B. 8   C. 4   D. 2

Answer ☐

23 How often does a MOT certificate have to be renewed for
vehicles over three years old?

A. Every 3 years   B. Every 2 years

C. Every 18 months   D. Every 12 months

Answer ☐

24 Anti-discrimination laws do not apply when the job involves working for someone in their own home.

A. True   B. False

Answer [   ]

Practice test 5

1 There are about 60 million people living in the UK.

A. True   B. False

Answer [   ]

2 The Huguenots came to Britain in the 16th and 18th centuries to escape religious persecution in which country?

A. Ireland   B. West Indies   C. France   D. India

Answer [   ]

3 In 1918 how old did a woman have to be to vote in a general election?

A. 21   B. 25   C. 30   D. 35

Answer [   ]

4 In which year did Britain admit 28,000 refugees from Uganda?

A. 1942   B. 1952   C. 1962   D. 1972

Answer [   ]

5 In Britain today, women's average hourly pay is 20% less than men's pay.

A. True   B. False

Answer [   ]

6 Which of these statements is correct?

A. 25% of children live with both birth parents.

B. 25% of children live in lone-parent families.

Answer [   ]

7   Which of these statements is correct?

A. 45% of all ethnic minority people live in the London area.

B. 45% of London's population are from the ethnic minorities.

Answer [   ]

8   There is no Great Britain football team.

A. True   B. False

Answer [   ]

9   In which parts of Scotland are you most likely to hear Gaelic spoken?

A. Dumfries and   B. Angus and
    Galloway   Dundee

C. Glasgow and   D. Highlands and
    Edinburgh   Islands

Answer [   ]

10 Who is the Supreme Governor of the Church of England?

A. Archbishop of   B. Prime
    Canterbury   Minister

C. Jesus Christ   D. The Queen

Answer [   ]

11 Which religion celebrates Eid ul-Fitr?

A. Jewish   B. Hindu

C. Muslim   D. Buddhist

Answer [   ]

12 On what night do children carry lanterns made out of pumpkins with a candle inside?

A. Burns' Night   B. New Year's Eve

C. Guy Fawkes' Night   D. Hallowe'en

Answer [   ]

13   In 1605, who tried to kill the Protestant king with a bomb in the Houses of Parliament?

A. Robert Burns

B. William Wallace

C. Guy Fawkes

D. Owain Glyndwr

Answer

14   In which country are A-levels known as Higher grades?

A. England

B. Wales

C. Scotland

D. Northern Ireland

Answer

15   Which Report publishes information about parliamentary debates?

A. Harvard

B. Hansard

C. Hazard

D. Hallam

Answer

16   Where does the Northern Ireland Assembly meet?

A. Stormont

B. Holyrood

C. Westminster

D. Senedd

Answer

17   Which of these statements is correct?

A. In 2006, there were 27 EU member countries.

B. In 2006, ten new member countries joined the EU.

Answer

18   Which of these statements is correct?

A. A landlord can change your rent at any time during the tenancy.

B. If you end a tenancy agreement early you are liable to pay the rent for the full period.

Answer

19   Which card draws money from your bank account?

A. Credit card   B. Store card

C. Cheque guarantee   D. Debit card
   card

Answer [   ]

20   Who writes out prescriptions for medication?

A. Pharmacist   B. General Practitioner

C. NHS Direct   D. Receptionist

Answer [   ]

21   What is the most number of hours a school child can spend delivering milk on any school day or on Sunday?

A. 12   B. 8   C. 4   D. 0

Answer [   ]

22   Which of these statements is correct?
A. It is legal for children aged 16 to buy tobacco.

B. It is legal for children aged 16 to sell tobacco.

Answer [   ]

23   At what age do UK citizens receive a National Insurance (NI) number to track their NI contributions?

A. 16   B. 18   C. 21   D. 65

Answer [   ]

24   Which TWO of the following make the best referees for a job application?

A. Previous   B. Members of
   employers   your family

C. Close   D. Professional
   friends   people

Answer [   ]

Practice test 6

1   The UK is made up of how many countries?

A. 1   B. 2   C. 4   D. 5

Answer [   ]

2   Which statement is correct?

A. Dental treatment is free on the NHS.

B. Most people have to pay for dental treatment.

Answer [   ]

3   Which one of the following is a public holiday?

A. 1st March in
   Wales

B. 17th March in
   Northern Ireland

C. 23rd April in
   England

D. 30th November
   in Scotland

Answer [   ]

4   A short letter attached to a completed job application form is what?

A. Curriculum vitae

B. Application letter

C. Covering letter

D. References

Answer [   ]

5   Why was immigration to the UK encouraged in the 1950s?

A. Political reasons

B. Promote multiculturalism

C. Religious grounds

D. Economic reasons

Answer [   ]

6   Which of these statements is correct?

A. School children take national tests in English, maths and science at ages 7 and 11.

B. School children take national tests in English, maths and science at age 16 and not before.

Answer [   ]

7 What percentage of UK children live within a stepfamily?

A. 10% B. 15% C. 20% D. 25%

Answer [   ]

8 Which one of the following is a very ancient festival?

A. Guy Fawkes' Night B. Remembrance Day

C. Mother's Day D. Hallowe'en

Answer [   ]

9 How many refugees from South East Asia has the UK admitted since the 1970s?

A. over 220 B. over 2,200

C. over 22,000 D. over 220,000

Answer [   ]

10 Which statement is correct?

A. All schools must provide their pupils with religious education (RE) lessons.

B. Parents are not allowed to withdraw their children from religious education (RE) lessons.

Answer [   ]

11 In Northern Ireland the law bans discrimination on the grounds of which one of the following?

A. Work experience B. CRB check

C. Political opinion D. Qualifications

Answer [   ]

12 What is the present voting age in all UK elections?

A. 21 B. 18 C. 17 D. 16

Answer [   ]

13 A live-in landlord can discriminate against you because of your sex, race, nationality or ethnic origin.

A. True   B. False

Answer [   ]

14 How many Black African people are there in the UK?

A. 0.1 million   B. 0.25 million   C. 0.5 million   D. 1 million

Answer [   ]

15 Tax is automatically taken from your earnings by

A. Department of Work and Pensions

B. HM Revenue & Customs

C. Department of Trade and Industry

D. HM Treasury

Answer [   ]

16 Which statement is correct?

A. The minimum wage is higher for 22 year olds than for 21 year olds.

B. The minimum wage is the same for 16 year olds and 18 year olds.

Answer [   ]

17 Which statement is correct?

A. The amount of council tax you pay depends on how much money you earn and take home.

B. The amount of council tax you pay depends on the size and value of your house or flat.

Answer [   ]

18 What letter number plate can a learner driver put on a car in Wales instead of an L-plate?

A. R-plate   B. D-plate   C. Q-plate   D. W-plate

Answer [   ]

19 Money from a university to help a student is called what?

A. Grant

B. Loan

C. Handout

D. Bursary

Answer

20 By what other name are Cabinet Ministers known?

A. Life Peers

B. Assembly Members

C. Secretaries
of State

D. Elected members

Answer

21 Council tax helps to pay for which TWO of the following?

A. Gas and electricity

B. Libraries

C. Roads

D. Water rates

Answer

22 Which one of the following does not provide information on social security benefits?

A. Jobcentre Plus

B. Post Offices

C. Credit union

D. Citizens Advice Bureau

Answer

23 Which one of the following is not a Commonwealth member?

A. Malawi

B. Malta

C. Mauritius

D. Madagascar

Answer

24 Which statement is correct?

A. A woman is entitled to maternity pay and it makes no difference how long she has worked for her employer.

B. A woman is entitled to 26 weeks maternity pay and it makes no difference how long she has worked for her employer.

Answer

CHAPTER 9

Answers

Blank marking sheet (✓ or ✗)

Chapter 1:   Practice test 1
(pass mark = 18 correct answers)

1	2	3	4	5	6
7	8	9	10	11	12
13	14	15	16	17	18
19	20	21	22	23	24

Chapter 2:   A changing society
(pass = 72 correct answers)

1	2	3	4	5	6
7	8	9	10	11	12
13	14	15	16	17	18

19	20	21	22	23	24
25	26	27	28	29	30
31	32	33	34	35	36
37	38	39	40	41	42
43	44	45	46	47	48
49	50	51	52	53	54
55	56	57	58	59	60
61	62	63	64	65	66
67	68	69	70	71	72
73	74	75	76	77	78
79	80	81	82	83	84
85	86	87	88	89	90
91	92	93	94	95	96

Chapter 3:   UK today: a profile (pass = 99 correct answers)

97	98	99	100	101	102
103	104	105	106	107	108
109	110	111	112	113	114
115	116	117	118	119	120
121	122	123	124	125	126
127	128	129	130	131	132
133	134	135	136	137	138
139	140	141	142	143	144
145	146	147	148	149	150
151	152	153	154	155	156
157	158	159	160	161	162
163	164	165	166	167	168

169	170	171	172	173	174
175	176	177	178	179	180
181	182	183	184	185	186
187	188	189	190	191	192
193	194	195	196	197	198
199	200	201	202	203	204
205	206	207	208	209	210
211	212	213	214	215	216
217	218	219	220	221	222
223	224	225	226	227	228

Chapter 4: How the UK is governed (pass = 90 correct answers)

229	230	231	232	233	234
235	236	237	238	239	240
241	242	243	244	245	246
247	248	249	250	251	252
253	254	255	256	257	258
259	260	261	262	263	264
265	266	267	268	269	270
271	272	273	274	275	276
277	278	279	280	281	282
283	284	285	286	287	288
289	290	291	292	293	294
295	296	297	298	299	300
301	302	303	304	305	306
307	308	309	310	311	312
313	314	315	316	317	318
319	320	321	322	323	324

325	326	327	328	329	330
331	332	333	334	335	336
337	338	339	340	341	342
343	344	345	346	347	348

Chapter 5: Everyday needs
(pass = 123 correct answers)

349	350	351	352	353	354
355	356	357	358	359	360
361	362	363	364	365	366
367	368	369	370	371	372
373	374	375	376	377	378
379	380	381	382	383	384
385	386	387	388	389	390
391	392	393	394	395	396
397	398	399	400	401	402
403	404	405	406	407	408
409	410	411	412	413	414
415	416	417	418	419	420
421	422	423	424	425	426
427	428	429	430	431	432
433	434	435	436	437	438
439	440	441	442	443	444
445	446	447	448	449	450
451	452	453	454	455	456
457	458	459	460	461	462
463	464	465	466	467	468
469	470	471	472	473	474
475	476	477	478	479	480

481	482	483	484	485	486
487	488	489	490	491	492
493	494	495	496	497	498
499	500	501	502	503	504
505	506	507	508	509	510
511	----	----	----	----	----

Chapter 6:   Employment
(pass = 53 correct answers)

512	513	514	515	516	517
518	519	520	521	522	523
524	525	526	527	528	529
530	531	532	533	534	535
536	537	538	539	540	541
542	543	544	545	546	547
548	549	550	551	552	553
554	555	556	557	558	559
560	561	562	563	564	565
566	567	568	569	570	571
572	573	574	575	576	577
578	579	580	581	----	----

Chapter 7:   Knowing the law

582	583	584	585	586	587
588	589	590	591	592	593
594	595	596	597	598	599
600	601	602	603	604	605
606	607	608	609	610	----

Chapter 8:   Practice tests 2 to 6
(pass = 18 correct answers)
Practice test 2

1	2	3	4	5	6
7	8	9	10	11	12
13	14	15	16	17	18
19	20	21	22	23	24

Practice test 3

1	2	3	4	5	6
7	8	9	10	11	12
13	14	15	16	17	18
19	20	21	22	23	24

Practice test 4

1	2	3	4	5	6
7	8	9	10	11	12
13	14	15	16	17	18
19	20	21	22	23	24

Practice test 5

1	2	3	4	5	6
7	8	9	10	11	12
13	14	15	16	17	18
19	20	21	22	23	24

Practice test 6

1	2	3	4	5	6
7	8	9	10	11	12
13	14	15	16	17	18
19	20	21	22	23	24

Answers

Chapter 1:   Practice test 1

1 A	2 A	3 A	4 D	5 B	6 D
7 C	8 D	9 A	10 B	11 C	12 A
13 C	14 C	15 D	16 B	17 CD	18 B
19 C	20 D	21 B	22 A	23 B	24 A

Chapter 2:   A changing society

1 A	2 A	3 B	4 A	5 B	6 A
7 BC	8 D	9 C	10 B	11 C	12 B
13 AD	14 D	15 A	16 D	17 A	18 CD
19 C	20 C	21 B	22 BC	23 D	24 C
25 BD	26 D	27 B	28 D	29 C	30 B
31 B	32 A	33 B	34 A	35 B	36 A
37 B	38 C	39 D	40 B	41 B	42 C
43 A	44 A	45 B	46 C	47 C	48 B
49 B	50 A	51 B	52 D	53 B	54 A
55 B	56 A	57 D	58 B	59 A	60 C
61 B	62 B	63 C	64 C	65 C	66 A
67 A	68 B	69 B	70 B	71 C	72 B
73 B	74 B	75 A	76 C	77 A	78 A

79 A	**80** B	**81** C	**82** A	**83** A	**84** B
85 B	**86** B	**87** B	**88** A	**89** A	**90** B
91 A	**92** B	**93** C	**94** B	**95** A	**96** D

5:   French Protestants

Chapter 3:   UK today: a profile

97 A	**98** B	**99** C	**100** D	**101** C	**102** B
103 A	**104** D	**105** A	**106** B	**107** B	**108** B
109 A	**110** D	**111** B	**112** B	**113** A	**114** C
115 D	**116** B	**117** D	**118** C	**119** B	**120** C
121 C	**122** C	**123** D	**124** A	**125** A	**126** C
127 B	**128** D	**129** B	**130** C	**131** A	**132** A
133 B	**134** D	**135** D	**136** C	**137** C	**138** A
139 A	**140** A	**141** D	**142** B	**143** B	**144** A
145 A	**146** D	**147** D	**148** B	**149** B	**150** B
151 A	**152** A	**153** B	**154** A	**155** C	**156** D
157 A	**158** A	**159** B	**160** B	**161** B	**162** C
163 D	**164** A	**165** A	**166** B	**167** D	**168** D
169 C	**170** B	**171** A	**172** B	**173** C	**174** AC
175 A	**176** B	**177** B	**178** A	**179** A	**180** C
181 B	**182** D	**183** C	**184** B	**185** A	**186** C
187 A	**188** D	**189** B	**190** A	**191** B	**192** D
193 A	**194** A	**195** B	**196** A	**197** A	**198** C
199 B	**200** B	**201** B	**202** A	**203** B	**204** A
205 A	**206** A	**207** B	**208** A	**209** A	**210** B
211 A	**212** C	**213** A	**214** A	**215** D	**216** D
217 B	**218** C	**219** A	**220** B	**221** B	**222** C
223 B	**224** B	**225** D	**226** A	**227** B	**228** D

116:   B: anonymous and confidential

Chapter 4: How the UK is governed

229 AC	**230** A	**231** B	**232** B	**233** A	**234** B
235 CD	**236** A	**237** B	**238** B	**239** C	**240** D
241 D	**242** D	**243** D	**244** A	**245** A	**246** A
247 D	**248** B	**249** C	**250** B	**251** A	**252** B
253 A	**254** C	**255** C	**256** C	**257** D	**258** C
259 B	**260** B	**261** C	**262** B	**263** B	**264** B
265 A	**266** B	**267** B	**268** A	**269** A	**270** A
271 D	**272** B	**273** B	**274** A	**275** A	**276** B
277 A	**278** C	**279** C	**280** B	**281** B	**282** B
283 D	**284** C	**285** A	**286** A	**287** B	**288** A
289 B	**290** A	**291** A	**292** D	**293** B	**294** A
295 A	**296** B	**297** A	**298** C	**299** C	**300** C
301 B	**302** A	**303** A	**304** B	**305** A	**306** B
307 B	**308** A	**309** B	**310** C	**311** A	**312** A
313 B	**314** B	**315** C	**316** A	**317** AD	**318** A
319 D	**320** A	**321** A	**322** B	**323** BC	**324** B
325 B	**326** D	**327** B	**328** C	**329** D	**330** D
331 A	**332** A	**333** A	**334** A	**335** A	**336** B
337 B	**338** B	**339** D	**340** BD	**341** A	**342** A
343 D	**344** B	**345** C	**346** B	**347** A	**348** D

Chapter 5: Everyday needs

349 C	**350** A	**351** BD	**352** A	**353** A	**354** C
355 C	**356** A	**357** B	**358** A	**359** B	**360** A
361 C	**362** B	**363** B	**364** A	**365** C	**366** A
367 A	**368** A	**369** B	**370** B	**371** A	**372** B
373 B	**374** A	**375** B	**376** A	**377** C	**378** A

379 A	**380** A	**381** A	**382** B	**383** B	**384** C
385 B	**386** BD	**387** B	**388** B	**389** A	**390** B
391 B	**392** A	**393** BC	**394** BD	**395** D	**396** B
397 AC	**398** B	**399** B	**400** D	**401** B	**402** B
403 A	**404** B	**405** C	**406** A	**407** AC	**408** A
409 B	**410** B	**411** B	**412** B	**413** B	**414** B
415 A	**416** A	**417** C	**418** A	**419** B	**420** A
421 A	**422** C	**423** A	**424** B	**425** A	**426** A
427 B	**428** B	**429** BD	**430** CD	**431** C	**432** C
433 A	**434** D	**435** A	**436** B	**437** B	**438** A
439 A	**440** A	**441** A	**442** A	**443** B	**444** A
445 B	**446** B	**447** B	**448** B	**449** B	**450** A
451 A	**452** A	**453** A	**454** A	**455** A	**456** B
457 BC	**458** A	**459** A	**460** B	**461** B	**462** A
463 A	**464** A	**465** B	**466** C	**467** A	**468** A
469 A	**470** B	**471** B	**472** B	**473** B	**474** A
475 B	**476** C	**477** B	**478** A	**479** B	**480** C
481 D	**482** A	**483** B	**484** B	**485** A	**486** A
487 A	**488** B	**489** D	**490** C	**491** A	**492** C
493 D	**494** B	**495** A	**496** A	**497** B	**498** B
499 B	**500** A	**501** B	**502** A	**503** B	**504** C
505 B	**506** C	**507** C	**508** B	**509** AD	**510** BC
511 D	----	----	----	----	

387:   B: no one pound note (coins only)
460:   B: aged 4 years and over

Chapter 6: Employment

512 D	**513** B	**514** D	**515** A	**516** B	**517** D
518 D	**519** BD	**520** C	**521** AB	**522** A	**523** B

524 A	**525** A	**526** B	**527** A	**528** A	**529** A
530 B	**531** D	**532** D	**533** B	**534** B	**535** B
536 A	**537** B	**538** A	**539** B	**540** A	**541** C
542 A	**543** A	**544** B	**545** B	**546** B	**547** A
548 C	**549** B	**550** BC	**551** AB	**552** A	**553** C
554 B	**555** C	**556** D	**557** B	**558** B	**559** BD
560 A	**561** A	**562** BC	**563** B	**564** B	**565** A
566 B	**567** B	**568** C	**569** B	**570** B	**571** B
572 A	**573** AC	**574** A	**575** B	**576** D	**577** D
578 A	**579** B	**580** AD	**581** B	----	----

Chapter 7:   Knowing the law

582 A	**583** B	**584** B	**585** A	**586** A	**587** AD
588 D	**589** B	**590** B	**591** D	**592** A	**593** D
594 A	**595** A	**596** C	**597** B	**598** A	**599** A
600 A	**601** B	**602** B	**603** A	**604** B	**605** B
606 B	**607** B	**608** B	**609** A	**610** A	----

604:   B: 18
606:   B: it is a guide to everyday law for people aged 14 to 19
608:   B: *7 days* not 28 days

Chapter 8:   Practice tests 2 to 6
Practice test 2

1 B	**2** B	**3** C	**4** B	**5** B	**6** A
7 C	**8** C	**9** A	**10** D	**11** C	**12** B
13 B	**14** B	**15** B	**16** D	**17** B	**18** B
19 A	**20** C	**21** BC	**22** B	**23** D	**24** B

Practice test 3

1 B	2 A	3 D	4 A	5 B	6 A
7 B	8 A	9 D	10 C	11 C	12 B
13 B	14 C	15 C	16 D	17 C	18 A
19 D	20 D	21 B	22 D	23 A	24 B

Practice test 4

1 A	2 A	3 C	4 C	5 D	6 B
7 D	8 A	9 B	10 C	11 A	12 C
13 C	14 D	15 A	16 B	17 B	18 C
19 D	20 B	21 A	22 D	23 D	24 A

Practice test 5

1 A	2 C	3 C	4 D	5 A	6 B
7 A	8 A	9 D	10 D	11 C	12 D
13 C	14 C	15 B	16 A	17 A	18 B
19 D	20 B	21 D	22 B	23 A	24 AD

17:   A: ten new members joined in 2004 not 2006

Practice test 6

1 C	2 B	3 B	4 C	5 D	6 A
7 A	8 D	9 C	10 A	11 C	12 B
13 A	14 C	15 B	16 A	17 B	18 B
19 D	20 C	21 BC	22 C	23 D	24 B

13:   A: true if shares the accommodation

Human rights

1 The right to life

2 Prohibition of torture

3 Prohibition of slavery and forced labour

4 The right to liberty and security

5 The right to a fair trial

6 No punishment without law

7 Right to respect a person's private and family life

8 Freedom of thought, conscience and religion

9 Freedom of expression

10 Freedom of assembly and association

11 Right to marry and have a family

12 Prohibition of discrimination

13 Protection of property

14 The right to education

15 The right to free elections

16 Prohibition of the death penalty

Commonwealth countries (53)

Antigua and Barbuda, Australia, The Bahamas, Bangladesh, Barbados, Belize, Botswana, Brunei Darussalam, Cameroon, Canada, Cyprus, Dominica, Fiji Islands, The Gambia, Ghana, Grenada, Guyana, India, Jamaica, Kenya, Kiribati, Lesotho, Malawi, Malaysia, Maldives, Malta, Mauritius, Mozambique, Namibia, Nauru, New Zealand, Nigeria, Pakistan, Papua New Guinea, St Kitts and Nevis, St Lucia, St Vincent and the Grenadines, Samoa, Seychelles, Sierra Leone, Singapore, Solomon Islands, South Africa, Sri Lanka, Swaziland, Tonga, Trinidad and Tobago, Tuvalu, Uganda, United Kingdom, United Republic of Tanzania, Vanuatu, Zambia.

Life in the UK website addresses

Taking the test: www.lifeintheuktest.gov.uk

Government: www.parliament.uk; www.statistics.gov.uk/census

Homelessness: www.shelternet.org.uk

Neighbours: www.mediation.co.uk

Credit unions: www.abcup.coop

Health and feeling unwell: www.nhs.uk;
   www.nhsdirect.nhs.uk (England and Wales);
   www.nhs24.com (Scotland);
   www.n-i.nhs.uk (Northern Ireland)

Contraception and sexual health: www.fpa.org.uk

Pregnancy: www.nctpregnancyandbabycare.com

Careers education: www.connexions-direct.com (England);
   www.careerswales.com (Wales);
   www.careers-scotland.org.uk (Scotland)

Further education: www.dfes.gov.uk

Pets: www.pdsa.org.uk (veterinary services)

Trains and coaches: www.nationalrail.co.uk;
www.nationalexpress.com; www.citylink.co.uk (Scotland);
www.translink.co.uk (Northern Ireland)

Qualifications: www.naric.org.uk

Criminal record: www.disclosurescotland.co.uk

Training: learndirect.co.uk

Volunteering: www.do-it.org.uk; www.volunteering.org.uk;
www.justdosomething.net; www.csv.org.uk;
www.princes-trust.org.uk

Charities: www.comicrelief.com; www.greenpeace.org.uk;
www.oxfam.org.uk; www.foe.org.uk; www.wwf.org.uk

Citizens Advice Bureaux: www.adviceguide.org.uk

Equal rights/discrimination: www.equalityhumanrights.com

Pensions and financial advice: www.opas.org.uk;
www.unbiased.co.uk

Work: www.workingintheuk.gov.uk; www.jobcentreplus.gov.uk;
www.newdeal.gov.uk

Problems at work: www.acas.org.uk; www.worksmart.org.uk;
www.tuc.org.uk

Children: www.childcarelink.gov.uk; ncma.org.uk;
www.parentlineplus.org.uk; www.bbc.co.uk/parenting;
www.childline.org.uk

Crime: www.online.police.uk; www.victimsupport.com

Solicitors: www.solicitors-online.com

Law and criminal injuries: www.clsdirect.org.uk;
www.lawcentres.org.uk; www.cica.gov.uk

Consumer rights: www.oft.gov.uk; www.bbc.co.uk

Yellow pages telephone directory: www.yell.com

Important dates
in history

1500s: Huguenots come to Britain to escape persecution.

1530s: Church of England established (Reformation).

1605: Guy Fawkes tries to blow up the Houses of Parliament.

1801: Date of the first census.

1840s: Irish people migrate to Britain to escape famine.

1857: Women can divorce their husbands.

1880: Jewish people come to Britain to escape 'pogroms'.

1882: Women who marry can keep their money and property.

1914: First World War begins.

1918: First World War ends.

1918: Women over age 30 are given the right to vote.

1922: Northern Ireland Parliament created.

1928: Women can vote at age 21, the same as men.

1939: Second World War begins.

1945: Second World War ends.

1948: National Health Service created.

1949: Council of Europe created; UK is a founder member.

1952: Queen Elizabeth II accedes to the throne.

1957: Treaty of Rome signed and EU created.

1969:   Voting age reduced to age 18.
1969:   Troubles break out in Northern Ireland.
1970s: Refugees admitted from Uganda and South East Asia.
1972:   Northern Ireland Parliament abolished.
1973:   UK joins the EU.
1999:   Welsh Assembly and Scottish Parliament formed.
2001:   Date of the last UK census.
2004:   Ten new member states join the EU.
2004:   Large numbers of people arrive from Eastern Europe.
2007:   Commission for Equality and Human Rights set up.
2011:   Date of next census (every 10 years).

Important dates in the UK calendar

1st January:	New Year's Day.
14th February:	St Valentine's Day.
1st March:	St David's Day in Wales.
17th March:	St Patrick's Day in Northern Ireland.
3 weeks before Easter:	Mother's Day.
1st April:	April Fool's Day.
23rd April:	St George's Day in England.
1st May:	May Day.
End of August Bank Holiday:	Notting Hill Carnival.
31st October:	Hallowe'en.
5th November:	Guy Fawkes' Night (Bonfire Night).
11th November:	Remembrance Day (Armistice Day).
30th November:	St Andrew's Day in Scotland.
24th December:	Christmas Eve.
25th December:	Christmas Day.
26th December:	Boxing Day (Bank Holiday).
31st December:	New Year's Eve (Hogmanay in Scotland).

Important abbreviations

ABCUL:	Association of British Credit Unions Limited.
ACAS:	Advisory, Conciliation and Arbitration Service.
A&E:	Accident and Emergency Department.
AGCE:	General Certificate of Education at an Advanced Level.
AMs:	Assembly Members (Welsh Assembly).
AS level:	Advanced Subsidiary qualification.
BT:	British Telecom.
CRB:	Criminal Records Bureau.
CV:	Curriculum vitae.
DWP:	Department for Work and Pensions.
EAL:	English as an Additional Language.
EEC:	European Economic Community.
EMA:	Education Maintenance Allowance.
ESOL:	English for Speakers of Other Languages.
EU:	European Union.
FA cup:	Football Association cup.
FE:	Further Education.
FPA:	Family Planning Association.
GB:	Great Britain.

GCSE: General Certificate of Secondary Education.
GP: General Practitioner.
HM: Her Majesty.
ICT: Information and communication technology.
ID card: Identity card.
JSA: Job Seeker's Allowance.
LGA: Local Government Association.
L-plates: Learner driver.
MEP: Member of the European Parliament.
MLAs: Members of the Legislative Assembly (N Ireland).
MOT: Ministry of Transport.
MP: Member of Parliament.
Mph: Miles per hour.
MSPs: Members of the Scottish Parliament.
NARIC: National Academic Recognition Centre.
NHS: National Health Service.
NI: National Insurance.
NIC: National Insurance Contribution.
PALS: Patient Advice and Liaison Service.
PE: Physical Education.
PIN: Personal Identification Number.
PM: Prime Minister.
PMQs: Prime Minister's Questions.
PSNI: Police Service for Northern Ireland.
TUC: Trades Union Congress.
TV: Television.
UK: United Kingdom.
UN: United Nations.
WAG: Welsh Assembly Government.
YPBA: Young Person's Bridging Allowance.

- *How to Pass Numeracy Tests*
- *How to Pass Numerical Reasoning Tests*
- *How to Pass Professional Level Psychometric Tests*
- *How to Pass the Police Selection System*
- *How to Pass the QTS Numeracy Skills Test*
- *How to Pass the UK's National Firefighter Selection Process*
- *How to Pass Verbal Reasoning Tests*
- *How to Succeed at an Assessment Centre*
- *IQ and Aptitude Tests*
- *IQ and Psychometric Tests*
- *The Numeracy Test Workbook*
- *Test your Emotional Intelligence*
- *Test and Assess Your Brain Quotient*
- *Ultimate Psychometric Tests*
- *Ultimate IQ Tests*

Careers

- *The A–Z of Careers and Jobs*
- *Career, Aptitude and Selection Tests*
- *Disaster Proof Your Career*
- *Great Answers to Tough Interview Questions*
- *How to Get into Medical School*
- *Knockout Job Interview Presentations*
- *Learn While You Earn*

- *Preparing the Perfect CV*
- *Preparing the Perfect Job Application*
- *Readymade CVs*
- *Readymade Job Search Letters*
- *The Redundancy Survival Guide*
- *The Study Skills Guide*
- *Succeed in your Medical School Interview*
- *Successful Interview Skills*
- *Ultimate CV*
- *Ultimate Cover Letters*
- *Ultimate Interview*
- *Ultimate Job Search*
- *What Next After School*

For more information go to www.koganpage.com.

Also available from **Kogan Page**

Find out more; visit **www.koganpage.com** and
sign up for offers and regular e-newsletters.

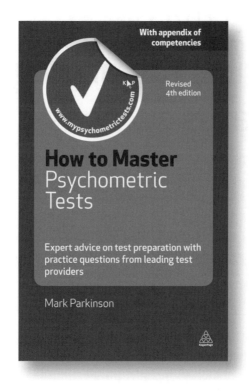

The sharpest minds need the finest advice. **Kogan Page** creates success.

www.koganpage.com